Better Homes and Gardens.

HOMEMADE COOKIES COOK BOOK

© 1975 by Meredith Corporation, Des Moines, Iowa.
All Rights Reserved. Printed in the United States of America.
Large-Format Edition. Third Printing, 1983.
Library of Congress Catalog Card Number: 74-75786
ISBN: 0-696-01140-9

On the cover: Bake up a batch of moist and flavor-packed bar cookies. The taste-tempting collection includes *Candy-Meringue Bars, Fruit Cocktail Bars,* chocolate-topped *Filbert Bars,* and *Apricot-Almond Bars.*

Above: Let the whole family join in the fun of Christmas preparations. Have each individual personalize giant-sized *Christmas Card Cookies* with messages to give as holiday greetings. (See Index for page numbers.)

Contents

BETTER HOMES AND GARDENS® BOOKS

Editorial Director: Don Dooley
Managing Editor: Malcolm E. Robinson   Art Director: John Berg
Asst. Managing Editor: Lawrence D. Clayton   Asst. Art Director: Randall Yontz
Food Editor: Nancy Morton
Senior Food Editor: Joyce Trollope
Associate Editors: Sharyl Heiken, Rosemary C. Hutchinson, Elizabeth Strait
Assistant Editors: Sandra Granseth, Catherine Penney
Designers: Faith Berven, Harijs Priekulis
Contributing Editor: Lorene Frohling

Our seal assures you that every recipe in the *Homemade Cookies Cook Book* is endorsed by the Better Homes and Gardens Test Kitchen. Each recipe is thoroughly tested for family appeal, practicality, and deliciousness.

Bar Cookie Treasure Chest

Bar cookies, with their rich flavor and moist texture, have long been popular as desserts and snacks. But today they are becoming even more of a favorite because busy homemakers appreciate their easy preparation. Just mix the ingredients, turn the dough into a baking pan, and in a short time you'll have cake-like cookies to serve at home or to enjoy anywhere. Bar cookies travel especially well in their own baking pan for away from home eating.

On the following pages you'll find a treasury of bar cookie recipes to please the heartiest of appetites. Many everyday bar cookies are featured here, as well as some fancier varieties that suit party occasions. There's even a whole section devoted to the immortal brownie—25 assorted kinds. For a time-saving bonus, try the quick cookie mixes you can partially make in advance and prepare cookies as needed.

Select from this treasury of bar cookies (clockwise, starting at left front): *Mint Swirl Brownies, Cheesecake Bars, Polka-Dot Angel Bars,* and *Hawaiian Fruit Bars.* (See Index for page numbers.)

6

Everyday Bar Cookies

Toffee Bars

½ cup butter *or* margarine, softened
½ cup sugar
½ teaspoon salt
1 cup all-purpose flour
1 14-ounce can *sweetened condensed* milk
2 tablespoons butter *or* margarine
¼ teaspoon salt
2 teaspoons vanilla
Fudge Frosting (see recipe, page 26)

Cream first 3 ingredients; stir in flour. Pat into ungreased 13x9x2-inch baking pan. Bake at 350° till lightly browned, about 15 minutes. In heavy saucepan stir condensed milk, 2 tablespoons butter, and ¼ teaspoon salt over low heat till butter melts. Cook and stir for 5 minutes over medium heat. (Mixture will thicken and become smooth.) Stir in vanilla. Spread over baked layer. Bake at 350° till golden, 12 to 15 minutes. Spread warm cookies with Fudge Frosting. While warm, cut into bars and remove from pan. Makes 48.

Pumpkin Bars

1 package 2-layer-size spice cake mix
½ cup butter *or* margarine, melted
3 eggs
1 cup canned pumpkin
½ cup sugar
½ teaspoon grated orange peel
½ cup chopped pecans

Reserve ⅔ cup dry cake mix. In large bowl combine remaining cake mix, butter, and *1* of the eggs; mix well. Pat into well-greased 13x9x2-inch baking pan. Bake at 350° for 15 minutes. Combine reserved cake mix, pumpkin, sugar, 2 eggs, peel, and dash salt. Beat at medium speed of electric mixer 1 to 2 minutes. Pour over partially baked layer. Top with nuts. Bake at 350° till set, 15 to 20 minutes. Cool; cut into bars. Refrigerate. Makes 32.

Cereal-Spice Bars

Keep extras on hand in the freezer—

Thoroughly stir together 1 package 2-layer-size spice cake mix, ½ cup quick-cooking rolled oats, and ¼ cup wheat germ. Beat 2 eggs; add ½ cup light molasses, ¼ cup milk, and ¼ cup cooking oil. Mix well. Stir into dry mixture; blend just till moistened. Stir in ½ cup shredded coconut. Spread in lightly greased 15½x10½x1-inch baking pan. Bake at 375° for 20 minutes. Cool; sift powdered sugar over. Cut into bars. Makes 60.

Maple-Walnut Bars

Pricking cookies lets glaze soak in readily—

¼ cup butter *or* margarine, softened
½ cup sugar
1 egg
½ teaspoon maple flavoring
1 cup all-purpose flour
½ teaspoon baking powder
½ teaspoon baking soda
½ cup milk
½ cup chopped walnuts
Maple Glaze

Cream butter and sugar till fluffy; beat in egg and flavoring. Stir together flour, baking powder, and soda; stir into creamed mixture alternately with milk. Stir in nuts. Spread in greased 11x7½x1½-inch baking pan. Bake at 350° for 20 to 25 minutes. Generously prick hot cookies with fork; slowly drizzle Maple Glaze over top. Cool; cut into bars. Makes 21.
Maple Glaze: Combine ⅔ cup sifted powdered sugar, ⅓ cup milk, and 3 tablespoons butter. Cook and stir till boiling. Remove from heat; add ½ teaspoon maple flavoring.

Quick and nutritious *Cereal-Spice Bars* get a speedy start with a spice cake mix. They're an especially good choice for busy homemakers.

TEST KITCHEN TIP

For an accurate measurement, spoon dry ingredients, such as all-purpose flour, granulated sugar, and powdered sugar, lightly into a measuring cup, then level off with a spatula or straight edge. Do not tap or shake the cup.

However, to measure brown sugar, firmly pack into a measuring cup so that the sugar retains its shape when turned out.

Nut Squares

In small mixing bowl beat 3 eggs till thick and lemon-colored. Gradually add ¾ cup granulated sugar; beat thoroughly. Blend in 1¼ teaspoons vanilla and ¼ teaspoon salt. Fold in 2 cups finely crushed graham crackers (28 square crackers) and ¼ cup chopped nuts. Turn mixture into greased 9x9x2-inch baking pan. Bake at 300° till done, 25 to 30 minutes. Cool thoroughly; sift powdered sugar over. Cut into squares. Makes 36.

Coconut-Peanut Butter Bars

Cream together ½ cup peanut butter, 6 tablespoons softened butter *or* margarine, and 1 cup sugar. Beat in 2 eggs and 1 teaspoon vanilla; mix well. Stir together 1 cup whole wheat flour, 1 teaspoon baking powder, and ¼ teaspoon salt; stir into creamed mixture with 1 cup flaked coconut. Spread in greased 11x7½x1½-inch baking pan. Bake at 350° for 25 to 30 minutes. Cool; cut into bars. Drizzle with Confectioners' Icing. Makes 24.

Confectioners' Icing: Stir together 1 cup sifted powdered sugar and enough light cream to make mixture of spreading consistency. Blend in ½ teaspoon vanilla and dash salt.

Cinnamon Diamonds

  1 cup butter *or* margarine, softened
  1 cup packed brown sugar
  1 egg yolk
  ½ teaspoon vanilla
  2 cups all-purpose flour
  1 teaspoon ground cinnamon
  1 slightly beaten egg white
  ¾ cup chopped walnuts

Cream butter and brown sugar; beat in egg yolk and vanilla. Stir together flour and cinnamon; stir into creamed mixture. Pat into ungreased 15½x10½x1-inch baking pan. Brush with egg white. Sprinkle with nuts; lightly press into top. Bake at 350° for 18 to 20 minutes. Cut into diamonds while warm. Makes 48.

Chocolate Revel Bars

   1 cup butter *or* margarine, softened
   2 cups packed brown sugar
   2 eggs
   2 teaspoons vanilla
   3 cups quick-cooking rolled oats
 2½ cups all-purpose flour
   1 teaspoon baking soda
 1½ teaspoons salt
   1 14-ounce can *sweetened condensed* milk
   1 12-ounce package semisweet chocolate pieces (2 cups)
   2 tablespoons butter *or* margarine
   1 cup chopped walnuts
   2 teaspoons vanilla

In large bowl cream together 1 cup butter and brown sugar till fluffy; beat in eggs and 2 teaspoons vanilla. Stir together oats, flour, soda, and *1 teaspoon* of the salt; stir into creamed mixture till blended. Set aside.

In heavy saucepan stir milk, chocolate, 2 tablespoons butter, and remaining ½ teaspoon salt over low heat till smooth. Remove from heat; stir in nuts and 2 teaspoons vanilla.

Pat ⅔ of the oat mixture into ungreased 15½x10½x1-inch baking pan. Spread chocolate mixture over oat layer; sprinkle with remaining oat mixture. Bake at 350° for 25 to 30 minutes. Cool; cut into bars. Makes 75.

Butterscotch Bars

½ cup butter *or* margarine
2 cups packed brown sugar
2 eggs
1 teaspoon vanilla
2 cups all-purpose flour
2 teaspoons baking powder
1 cup shredded coconut
1 cup chopped walnuts

In 2-quart saucepan melt butter or margarine over low heat. Remove from heat; stir in brown sugar. Add eggs, one at a time, beating well after each addition. Stir in vanilla.

Stir together flour, baking powder, and ¼ teaspoon salt. Add to brown sugar mixture with coconut and nuts; mix well. Spread in greased 15½x10½x1-inch baking pan. Bake at 350° about 25 minutes. Cut into bars while warm; remove from pan when cool. Makes 36.

Saucepan Taffy Bars

These chewy, molasses-flavored bars (shown on page 89) are ideal for gift-giving—

½ cup shortening
⅓ cup light molasses
¾ cup packed brown sugar
1 egg
1¼ cups all-purpose flour
¼ teaspoon baking soda
⅓ cup chopped walnuts
Lemon-Butter Frosting

In saucepan heat shortening and molasses to boiling. Remove from heat; stir in brown sugar. In mixing bowl beat egg; beat in molasses mixture till fluffy. Stir together flour, soda, and ½ teaspoon salt; stir into molasses mixture. Blend in nuts. Spread in greased 9x9x2-inch baking pan. Bake at 350° for 20 to 25 minutes. Cool; spread with Lemon-Butter Frosting. Cut into bars. Makes 24.

Lemon-Butter Frosting: Cream 1½ tablespoons softened butter or margarine and ⅛ teaspoon grated lemon peel. Gradually blend in ½ cup sifted powdered sugar. Beat in 1 tablespoon lemon juice and ¼ teaspoon vanilla. Gradually blend in ½ to ¾ cup sifted powdered sugar till of spreading consistency.

Caramel-Frosted Bars

See footnote on page 25 for toasting nuts—

6 tablespoons butter *or* margarine, softened
¾ cup granulated sugar
1 egg
2 tablespoons milk
¾ teaspoon vanilla
1¼ cups all-purpose flour
½ teaspoon baking soda
½ teaspoon salt
¼ cup chopped almonds *or* pecans, toasted
⅓ cup packed brown sugar
2 tablespoons butter *or* margarine
2 tablespoons water
1 teaspoon vanilla
1 cup sifted powdered sugar
2 tablespoons chopped almonds *or* pecans, toasted

Cream first 2 ingredients. Beat in egg, milk, and ¾ teaspoon vanilla. Stir flour with soda and salt; add to creamed mixture. Mix well. Stir in ¼ cup nuts. Spread in greased 9x9x2-inch baking pan. Bake at 375° for 20 to 25 minutes.

In saucepan combine brown sugar, 2 tablespoons butter, and water. Bring to a boil; stir constantly. Remove from heat; stir in 1 teaspoon vanilla. Gradually stir in powdered sugar. (If too thick, add a few drops hot water till of spreading consistency.) Stir in 2 tablespoons nuts. Immediately spread over warm cookies. Cut into bars. Makes 24.

TEST KITCHEN TIP

Cool bar cookies before frosting unless specified otherwise. To frost, spread icing evenly with a spatula over top of cookies to edges of baking pan.

Fig Bars

½ cup butter *or* margarine, softened
1 cup packed brown sugar
3 eggs
1 teaspoon grated lemon peel
1 teaspoon vanilla
1 cup all-purpose flour
1 teaspoon baking powder
½ teaspoon salt
1½ cups finely chopped dried figs

Cream butter and sugar. Add eggs, peel, and vanilla; beat well. Stir together flour, baking powder, and salt; blend into creamed mixture. Stir in figs. Pour into greased 13x9x2-inch baking pan. Bake at 350° for 25 minutes. Cool; cut into bars. Makes 32.

Raisin-Filled Cereal Bars
Sure to be a favorite with raisin fans—

Raisin Filling
¾ cup butter *or* margarine, softened
1 cup packed brown sugar
2 cups all-purpose flour
½ teaspoon baking soda
1½ cups granola cereal

Prepare Raisin Filling; cool. Cream butter and sugar. Stir together flour and soda. Add to creamed mixture with granola; mix well. (Mixture will be crumbly.) Pat *half* into greased and floured 13x9x2-inch baking pan. Spread with filling. Add 1 tablespoon water to remaining crumb mixture; sprinkle atop filling. Lightly press with hand. Bake at 350° for 30 to 35 minutes. Cut into bars while warm. Makes 32.

Raisin Filling: Mix ½ cup granulated sugar and 1 tablespoon cornstarch. Stir in 2 cups raisins and 1 cup water. Cook and stir over medium heat till thickened and bubbly. Remove from heat; stir in 2 tablespoons lemon juice.

◀ **Pack up a few bar cookies** when preparing family lunches. Cookies that can be carried include (clockwise, starting at lower left) *Caramel-Coconut Squares, Fig Bars, Apple-Spice Bars,* and layered *Raisin-Filled Cereal Bars.*

Chocolate Chip Bars
A soft bar cookie that children will love—

Cream ½ cup softened butter *or* margarine and ¾ cup packed brown sugar. Add 1 egg, 1 tablespoon milk, and 1 teaspoon vanilla; beat well. Stir together 1 cup all-purpose flour, ½ teaspoon baking powder, and ⅛ teaspoon *each* baking soda and salt. Add to creamed mixture; beat well. Stir in one 6-ounce package semisweet chocolate pieces. Spread in greased 9x9x2-inch baking pan. Bake at 350° for 30 to 35 minutes. Cool; cut into bars. Makes 32.

Caramel-Coconut Squares
Cookies will firm up as they cool—

½ cup butter *or* margarine, softened
½ cup sifted powdered sugar
1 cup all-purpose flour
1 14-ounce can *sweetened condensed* milk
1 6-ounce package butterscotch pieces
1 3½-ounce can flaked coconut (1⅓ cups)
1 teaspoon vanilla

Cream butter and sugar till fluffy; add flour and mix well. Pat into ungreased 9x9x2-inch baking pan. Bake at 350° for 12 to 15 minutes. Combine milk, butterscotch pieces, coconut, and vanilla; spread over partially baked layer. Bake at 350° till golden brown around edges, 25 to 30 minutes. (Cookies will not appear set.) Cool; cut into squares. Makes 36.

Apple-Spice Bars
Cake-like texture makes this cookie different—

Cream ⅓ cup shortening and ¾ cup sugar. Add 2 eggs; beat well. Stir together ¾ cup all-purpose flour, ½ teaspoon salt, ½ teaspoon baking powder, ¼ teaspoon baking soda, ¼ teaspoon ground nutmeg, and ¼ teaspoon ground ginger. Blend into creamed mixture; mix well. Stir in 1 cup finely chopped peeled apple. Spread in greased 13x9x2-inch baking pan. Sprinkle a mixture of 2 tablespoons sugar and ½ teaspoon ground cinnamon atop. Bake at 350° for 25 to 30 minutes. Cool; cut into bars. Makes 36.

Burnt Sugar Bars

Burnt Sugar Syrup
½ cup butter *or* margarine
1¼ cups granulated sugar
2 eggs
1 teaspoon vanilla
2¼ cups all-purpose flour
2 teaspoons baking powder
¼ teaspoon salt
½ cup chopped nuts
1 cup sifted powdered sugar
1 tablespoon butter *or* margarine, melted
Milk

Prepare Burnt Sugar Syrup; cool. In 2-quart saucepan melt ½ cup butter over low heat. Remove from heat; stir in granulated sugar. Add eggs, one at a time; beat well after each. Stir in vanilla and 3 *tablespoons* of the Burnt Sugar Syrup. Stir together flour, baking powder, and salt; stir into egg mixture. Stir in nuts. Spread in greased 15½x10½x1-inch baking pan. Bake at 350° for 13 to 15 minutes.

Combine powdered sugar, 1 tablespoon butter, and remaining Burnt Sugar Syrup. Add enough milk till of spreading consistency. Spread mixture over warm cookies. Cool thoroughly; cut into bars. Makes 48 bars.

Burnt Sugar Syrup: In heavy skillet melt ½ cup granulated sugar over low heat; stir constantly. Remove from heat when syrup is golden brown. Slowly add ½ cup boiling water; return to heat. Cook and stir till sugar dissolves. Boil to reduce to ⅓ cup, about 5 minutes.

Chewy Hermit Bars

Cream ½ cup shortening and ¾ cup packed brown sugar till fluffy; blend in 2 eggs, one at a time, beating well after each. Add ½ cup molasses; beat well. Stir together 1½ cups all-purpose flour, ¾ teaspoon ground cinnamon, ½ teaspoon baking soda, ½ teaspoon ground nutmeg, ½ teaspoon ground cloves, and ¼ teaspoon salt. Stir into creamed mixture.

Stir in 1½ cups raisins and ½ cup chopped walnuts. Spread in greased 13x9x2-inch baking pan. Bake at 350° for 25 to 30 minutes.

Cool slightly; sift powdered sugar over top. Cool thoroughly; cut into bars. Makes 32.

Spicy Raisin Bars

⅓ cup shortening
1 cup packed brown sugar
½ cup water
1 egg
1 teaspoon instant coffee crystals
1½ cups all-purpose flour
½ teaspoon baking powder
½ teaspoon ground cinnamon
¼ teaspoon baking soda
¼ teaspoon ground nutmeg
1 cup raisins

• • •

1 cup sifted powdered sugar
2 tablespoons butter *or* margarine, softened
1 tablespoon milk
¼ teaspoon vanilla
Dash salt

Cream shortening and brown sugar; add water, egg, and coffee crystals. Mix well. Stir flour with next 4 ingredients; slowly add to creamed mixture beating at low speed of electric mixer. Stir in raisins. Spread in greased 13x9x2-inch baking pan. Bake at 350° for 25 minutes.

Combine powdered sugar and remaining ingredients; mix thoroughly. Spread over slightly cooled cookies. Cool; cut into bars. Makes 40.

Apple Butter-Oatmeal Bars

½ cup butter *or* margarine, softened
½ cup packed brown sugar
½ cup apple butter
1 egg
⅔ cup all-purpose flour
½ teaspoon baking soda
½ teaspoon baking powder
¼ teaspoon salt
1 cup quick-cooking rolled oats
1 cup flaked coconut

Cream butter and sugar; blend in apple butter and egg. Stir flour with soda, baking powder, and salt; stir into creamed mixture. Stir in oats and coconut. Spread in greased 13x9x2-inch baking pan. Bake at 350° about 20 minutes. If desired, sift powdered sugar over top while warm; cool. Cut into bars. Makes 36.

Molasses-Ginger Bars

Gingerbread-flavored bars dotted with raisins—

½ cup butter *or* margarine, softened
½ cup packed brown sugar
½ cup molasses
1 egg
• • •
1½ cups all-purpose flour
1½ teaspoons baking powder
1 teaspoon ground ginger
½ teaspoon salt
¼ teaspoon baking soda
⅓ cup water
½ cup raisins
Powdered sugar

In mixing bowl cream together softened butter or margarine and brown sugar till mixture is fluffy. Add molasses and egg; beat well.

Thoroughly stir together flour, baking powder, ginger, salt, and baking soda. Add dry ingredients to creamed mixture alternately with water; mix well. Stir in raisins.

Pour mixture into greased 13x9x2-inch baking pan. Bake at 350° for 20 to 25 minutes. Cool thoroughly; sift powdered sugar over top. Cut into bars. Makes 36.

Banana-Chip Bars

¾ cup butter *or* margarine, softened
⅔ cup granulated sugar
⅔ cup packed brown sugar
1 egg
1 teaspoon vanilla
2 ripe medium bananas, mashed (1 cup)
• • •
2 cups all-purpose flour
2 teaspoons baking powder
½ teaspoon salt
1 6-ounce package semisweet chocolate
   pieces (1 cup)

Cream butter and sugars till fluffy. Add egg and vanilla; beat well. Stir in banana. Stir together flour, baking powder, and salt. Add to creamed mixture; beat well. Stir in chocolate pieces. Spread in greased and floured 15½x10½x1-inch baking pan. Bake at 350° for 25 minutes. Cool; cut into bars. Makes 36.

Peanut Butter-Oatmeal Bars

⅔ cup all-purpose flour
½ cup packed brown sugar
¼ teaspoon baking soda
¼ cup peanut butter
3 tablespoons shortening
1 beaten egg
1 tablespoon milk
½ teaspoon vanilla
¼ cup quick-cooking rolled oats
Peanut Butter Frosting

Stir together flour, sugar, soda, and ⅛ teaspoon salt; cut in peanut butter and shortening till mixture resembles coarse crumbs. Mix egg, milk, and vanilla; add to flour mixture with oats. Mix well. Spread in lightly greased 8x8x2-inch baking pan. Bake at 375° for 12 to 15 minutes. Cool; spread with Peanut Butter Frosting. Cut into bars. Makes 24.

Peanut Butter Frosting: Combine ¾ cup sifted powdered sugar, 1 tablespoon softened butter *or* margarine, and 1 tablespoon peanut butter. Blend in enough milk (2 to 3 teaspoons) till frosting is of spreading consistency.

Coffee-Apple Bars

Serve with ice cream for a special dessert—

In saucepan combine ½ cup raisins, ½ cup water, and 1 tablespoon instant coffee crystals; bring to boil. Remove from heat; let stand 5 minutes. Cream ¼ cup shortening and 1 cup packed brown sugar till fluffy; blend in 1 egg and 1 teaspoon vanilla. Stir together 1½ cups all-purpose flour, ½ teaspoon baking powder, ½ teaspoon baking soda, ½ teaspoon salt, and ½ teaspoon ground cinnamon. Add alternately with raisins to creamed mixture; mix well. Stir in 1 cup finely chopped peeled apple.

Spread in greased 13x9x2-inch baking pan. Bake at 350° for 25 to 30 minutes. Prepare Brown Sugar Icing; immediately spread over warm cookies. Cool; cut into bars. Makes 36.

Brown Sugar Icing: Combine ¼ cup packed brown sugar, 3 tablespoons butter *or* margarine, and 2 tablespoons milk. Cook and stir to boiling; remove from heat. Add ½ teaspoon vanilla. Slowly beat in sifted powdered sugar (about 1 cup) till of spreading consistency.

Basic Cookie Mix

*Use this mix to make the cookies found on this
page. Additional recipes are given on page 38—*

    4 cups all-purpose flour
    2 cups sugar
    2 teaspoons baking powder
    1½ teaspoons salt
    1⅓ cups shortening that does not
        require refrigeration

In large bowl thoroughly stir together first 4
ingredients. Cut in shortening till mixture resembles coarse cornmeal. Store in covered
container up to 6 weeks at room temperature.
For longer storage, place in freezer. To measure, lightly spoon mix into measuring cup;
level with spatula. Makes about 8½ cups.

Mince-Oatmeal Bars

A jiffy layered bar with a mincemeat filling—

    2 cups Basic Cookie Mix
    ¾ cup quick-cooking rolled oats
    1 beaten egg
    1 tablespoon water
    1 cup prepared mincemeat
    1 cup sifted powdered sugar
    ¼ teaspoon ground ginger
      Milk

Combine first 4 ingredients; pat *half* of the
mixture in greased 9x9x2-inch baking pan.
Spoon mincemeat over base; finely crumble
remaining oat mixture atop mincemeat. Bake
at 350° for 30 to 35 minutes. Mix sugar and
ginger; stir in enough milk (2 to 3 tablespoons)
till of drizzling consistency. Drizzle over warm
cookies. Cool; cut into bars. Makes 24.

Granola-Raisin Bars

In bowl combine 2 cups Basic Cookie Mix, ⅓
cup milk, 1 beaten egg, and ½ teaspoon vanilla;
beat well. Stir in ½ cup granola cereal and ½
cup raisins. Spread in greased 9x9x2-inch
baking pan. Combine ½ cup granola cereal
and 2 tablespoons butter *or* margarine, melted;
sprinkle over top. Bake at 350° for 20 to 25
minutes. Cool; cut into bars. Makes 24.

**TEST
KITCHEN
TIP**

Pour melted caramels over chocolate
chips for candy-topped *Chocolate-Cara-
mel Bars.* Carefully spread caramel mixture with spatula; chill before cutting.

Chocolate-Caramel Bars

    2 cups Basic Cookie Mix
    ½ cup milk
    1 beaten egg
    1 teaspoon vanilla
    ½ cup semisweet chocolate pieces
    16 vanilla caramels
    ¼ cup milk
    2 tablespoons chopped nuts

In mixing bowl combine first 4 ingredients;
beat well. Spread in greased 9x9x2-inch baking pan. Bake at 350° for 15 to 20 minutes.
Sprinkle chocolate pieces over warm base.

  In top of double boiler over *hot, not boiling
water* melt caramels in ¼ cup milk; stir till
smooth. Carefully pour atop chocolate; spread
evenly. Top with nuts. Chill about 2 hours;
cut into bars. Store in refrigerator. Makes 24.

Peanut-Molasses Bars

    2 cups Basic Cookie Mix
    1 beaten egg
    ¼ cup light molasses
    ½ cup chopped peanuts
    2 tablespoons water

In mixing bowl combine mix, egg, molasses,
¼ *cup* of the nuts, and water; mix well. Spread
in greased 9x9x2-inch baking pan. Top with
remaining nuts. Bake at 350° for 25 to 30
minutes. Cool; cut into bars. Makes 24.

Scotch Teas

1 cup packed brown sugar
½ cup butter *or* margarine
2 cups quick-cooking rolled oats
1 teaspoon baking powder

In saucepan combine sugar and butter; cook and stir till butter melts. Remove from heat; stir in oats, baking powder, and ¼ teaspoon salt. Mix well. Turn into greased 8x8x2-inch baking pan. Bake at 350° for 20 to 25 minutes. (Cookies will not appear set, but will harden upon cooling.) Cool; cut into bars. Makes 24.

Chocolate-Coconut Bars

1 14-ounce can *sweetened condensed* milk
1½ cups finely crushed graham crackers (21 square crackers)
1 3½-ounce can flaked coconut (1⅓ cups)
½ cup semisweet chocolate pieces

Combine all ingredients. Spread in well-greased and floured 8x8x2-inch baking pan. Bake at 350° for 30 minutes. Cool 10 minutes; remove from pan. Cool; cut into bars. Makes 32.

Coconut Chews

½ cup butter *or* margarine
1 package 2-layer-size white cake mix
¼ cup milk
1 3½-ounce can flaked coconut
1 12¼-ounce jar caramel topping (1 cup)
¼ cup all-purpose flour

In large bowl cut butter into cake mix till fine; carefully stir in milk. (Mixture will be crumbly; do not overmix.) Reserve *1 cup* mixture; firmly pat remaining mixture into ungreased 13x9x2-inch baking pan. Bake at 350° for 15 minutes. Top with coconut. Combine caramel topping and flour; heat through. Drizzle over coconut. Sprinkle with reserved crumb mixture. Bake 20 to 25 minutes longer. Cut into bars and remove from pan while warm. Makes 48.

Choco-Nut Refrigerator Bars

¾ cup butter *or* margarine
1 cup sugar
2 beaten eggs
2½ cups finely crushed graham crackers (35 square crackers)
2 cups tiny marshmallows
1 teaspoon vanilla
1 6-ounce package semisweet chocolate pieces (1 cup)
¼ cup peanut butter
¼ cup peanuts, finely chopped

In saucepan melt butter over low heat; remove from heat. Blend in sugar, then eggs; return to low heat. Cook and stir till thickened and bubbly; cool. Stir in graham crackers, marshmallows, and vanilla. Spread in well-buttered 9x9x2-inch baking pan. Chill.

In saucepan melt chocolate with peanut butter over low heat; stir constantly. Spread over cookies; sprinkle with peanuts. Chill thoroughly; cut into bars. Makes 36.

Crunchy Chocolate Bars

Use same cereal mixture to make drop cookies—

In saucepan combine one 12-ounce package semisweet chocolate pieces (2 cups) and ¾ cup chunk-style peanut butter. Stir over low heat till melted and smooth.

Remove from heat; stir in 3 cups round oat cereal. Turn into waxed paper-lined 8x8x2-inch baking pan; chill. Cut into bars. Makes 36.

Ginger-Mincemeat Bars

1 package gingerbread mix
1 cup prepared mincemeat
¼ cup water
1 can ready-to-spread lemon frosting
Sliced gumdrops

In mixing bowl combine dry gingerbread mix, prepared mincemeat, and water; beat smooth. Spread in greased 13x9x2-inch baking pan. Bake at 350° for 25 to 30 minutes. Cool. Spread with lemon frosting; cut into bars. Decorate with sliced gumdrops. Makes 24.

Festive Bar Cookies

Lemon Bars

1 cup all-purpose flour
¼ cup sifted powdered sugar
½ cup butter *or* margarine
2 eggs
¾ cup granulated sugar
½ teaspoon shredded lemon peel
3 tablespoons lemon juice
2 tablespoons all-purpose flour
¼ teaspoon baking powder
   Powdered sugar

Stir together 1 cup flour and ¼ cup powdered sugar; cut in butter till mixture clings together. Pat into ungreased 8x8x2-inch baking pan. Bake at 350° for 10 to 12 minutes.

In mixer bowl beat eggs; add granulated sugar, lemon peel, and juice. Beat till slightly thick and smooth, 8 to 10 minutes. Stir together 2 tablespoons flour and baking powder; add to egg mixture. Blend just till all is moistened. Pour over baked layer. Bake at 350° for 20 to 25 minutes. Sift powdered sugar over top. Cool; cut into bars. Makes 20.

Black Walnut Fingers

For best results, serve the same day as baked—

6 tablespoons butter, softened
1 cup packed brown sugar
1 teaspoon vanilla
1 egg yolk
¾ cup all-purpose flour
1 teaspoon baking powder
¼ teaspoon salt
½ cup chopped black walnuts
1 egg white
¼ cup packed brown sugar

Cream butter, 1 cup sugar, and vanilla; beat in egg yolk. Stir together flour, baking powder, and salt. Add to creamed mixture; mix well. Stir in ⅓ *cup* of the nuts. Pat into greased 11x7½x1½-inch baking pan. Bake at 325° for 15 minutes. Cool 5 minutes.

Meanwhile, beat egg white till soft peaks form; gradually add ¼ cup sugar, beating to stiff peaks. Fold in remaining nuts. Carefully spread over baked layer. Bake at 325° for 15 minutes. Cool; cut into bars. Makes 24.

Raspberry Bars

½ cup butter *or* margarine, softened
1 cup packed brown sugar
1½ cups all-purpose flour
½ teaspoon salt
½ teaspoon baking soda
1½ cups quick-cooking rolled oats
   • • •
1 teaspoon lemon juice
⅔ cup raspberry jam

Cream butter and sugar till fluffy. Stir together flour, salt, and soda; stir into creamed mixture. Add oats and ¼ cup water; mix till crumbly. Firmly pat *half* of the mixture into greased 13x9x2-inch baking pan. Stir lemon juice into jam; spread over base. Sprinkle with remaining crumb mixture. Bake at 350° for 25 minutes. Cool; cut into bars. Makes 40.

Cherry-Almond Bars

½ cup butter *or* margarine, softened
⅓ cup sifted powdered sugar
¼ teaspoon salt
1 cup all-purpose flour
½ cup almond paste, crumbled
1 3-ounce package cream cheese, softened
1 egg
½ cup red maraschino cherries, chopped

Cream butter, powdered sugar, and salt; stir in flour till mixture is crumbly. Pat into ungreased 9x9x2-inch baking pan. Bake at 350° for 12 to 15 minutes. Cream together almond paste and cream cheese till smooth. Add egg; mix well. Stir in cherries. Spread over baked layer. Bake at 350° till done, about 15 minutes. Cool; cut into bars. Makes 24.

Rich with brown sugar and nuts, *Chewy Noels* add a seasonal greeting to the holiday table. Change the message to fit the celebration with colorful decorator icing. It offers a quick and easy way to inscribe festive notes, dates, or names on cookies and party desserts.

Chewy Noels

    2 tablespoons butter *or* margarine
    1 cup packed brown sugar
    1 cup chopped nuts
    ⅓ cup all-purpose flour
    ⅛ teaspoon baking soda
    ⅛ teaspoon salt
    2 beaten eggs
    1 teaspoon vanilla
      Powdered sugar

In 9x9x2-inch baking pan melt butter or margarine. Stir together brown sugar, nuts, flour, soda, and salt; stir in eggs and vanilla. Carefully pour over butter in pan; do not stir. Bake at 350° for 20 to 25 minutes. Sift powdered sugar over top. Place waxed paper under wire rack; immediately invert pan onto rack. Cool. Dust again with powdered sugar. Cut into bars. Write Noel on each bar with green decorator icing, if desired. Makes 24.

Almond Cookie Strips

Cinnamon is subtle in meringue layer—

    1 cup butter *or* margarine, softened
    1 cup sugar
    1 egg yolk
    1 teaspoon vanilla
      Few drops almond extract
    2 cups all-purpose flour
    1 egg white
    2 tablespoons sugar
    ¼ teaspoon ground cinnamon
    ½ cup finely chopped almonds

Cream butter and 1 cup sugar till fluffy. Blend in egg yolk, vanilla, almond extract, and ⅛ teaspoon salt. Stir in flour; mix well. Pat into 15½x10½x1-inch baking pan. Beat egg white till stiff; beat in 2 tablespoons sugar and cinnamon. Fold in almonds; spread over base. Bake at 350° for 25 to 30 minutes. While warm, cut into bars. Makes 60.

Chewy Currant Bars

1 cup butter *or* margarine
¾ cup granulated sugar
¾ cup packed brown sugar
2 eggs
1 teaspoon shredded orange
    peel (set aside)
¼ cup orange juice
3 cups all-purpose flour
½ teaspoon baking soda
½ teaspoon salt
½ teaspoon ground cinnamon
¼ teaspoon ground cloves
1 cup dried currants
1 cup flaked coconut
¾ cup sifted powdered sugar
4 teaspoons orange juice

In saucepan melt butter over low heat; remove from heat. Stir in granulated and brown sugars. Add eggs, one at a time; beat well after each. Blend in ¼ cup orange juice. Mix flour with soda, salt, cinnamon, and cloves; stir into egg mixture. Fold in currants and coconut. Spread in greased 15½x10½x1-inch baking pan. Bake at 350° about 25 minutes. Combine powdered sugar, the 1 teaspoon shredded orange peel, and 4 teaspoons orange juice. Drizzle over warm cookies. Cool; cut into bars. Makes 48.

Cranberry Relish Squares

In saucepan combine ½ cup granulated sugar, 4 teaspoons cornstarch, and ½ teaspoon ground ginger; stir in one 14-ounce jar cranberry-orange relish. Stir over medium heat till bubbly; cook and stir 3 minutes more. Remove from heat; stir in ¾ cup chopped nuts. Cool.

Cream ½ cup softened butter *or* margarine and 1 cup packed brown sugar. Stir together 1½ cups all-purpose flour, ½ teaspoon baking soda, and ½ teaspoon salt; stir into creamed mixture. Add 1½ cups quick-cooking rolled oats and 1 tablespoon water; mix till crumbly.

Firmly pat *half* of the oat mixture into ungreased 13x9x2-inch baking pan. Spread with cranberry mixture. Combine remaining oat mixture and 1 tablespoon water; sprinkle over fruit. Pat smooth. Bake at 350° about 30 minutes. Cool; cut into squares. Makes 48.

Pineapple Preserve Bars

¾ cup butter *or* margarine, softened
1 cup sugar
1 egg
½ cup pineapple preserves
2 cups all-purpose flour
1 teaspoon baking soda
½ teaspoon salt
½ cup chopped nuts
    Pineapple Frosting

Cream butter and sugar till fluffy; beat in egg and preserves. Stir together flour, soda, and salt; stir into creamed mixture. Fold in nuts. Spread in greased 13x9x2-inch baking pan. Bake at 350° about 30 minutes. Cool slightly; spread with Pineapple Frosting. Cool thoroughly; cut into bars. Makes 32.

Pineapple Frosting: Blend 1¼ cups sifted powdered sugar, 2 tablespoons softened butter *or* margarine, and 2 tablespoons pineapple preserves till smooth. Add enough milk (about 1 tablespoon) till of spreading consistency.

Polka-Dot Angel Bars

A cake-type bar shown on pages 4 and 5—

4 egg whites
½ teaspoon cream of tartar
½ teaspoon vanilla
¾ cup sugar
¾ cup sifted cake flour
1 teaspoon baking powder
3 tablespoons cooking oil
1 5¾-ounce package milk chocolate
    pieces (1 cup)
½ cup chopped nuts
1 1-ounce square semisweet chocolate
½ teaspoon shortening

Beat first 3 ingredients till soft peaks form. Gradually add ½ *cup* of the sugar; beat to stiff peaks. Stir flour with remaining sugar, baking powder, and ¼ teaspoon salt. Fold into whites, 2 tablespoons at a time. Fold in oil, then chocolate pieces, and nuts. Spread in greased and waxed paper-lined 13x9x2-inch baking pan. Bake at 325° about 30 minutes. Melt chocolate square with shortening; drizzle over warm cookies. Cool; cut into bars. Makes 24.

Cardamom-Coffee Bars

       2 teaspoons instant coffee cyrstals
     ½ cup milk
     ¼ cup butter *or* margarine, softened
       1 cup granulated sugar
       1 egg
    1½ cups all-purpose flour
       1 teaspoon baking powder
     ½ teaspoon ground cardamom
     ¼ teaspoon baking soda
     ¼ teaspoon salt
       1 cup chopped nuts
       1 cup sifted powdered sugar
         Milk

Dissolve coffee crystals in ½ cup milk; set aside. Cream butter and granulated sugar; beat in egg. Stir flour with baking powder, cardamom, soda, and salt. Add alternately with coffee-milk mixture to creamed mixture. Stir in nuts. Spread in greased 13x9x2-inch baking pan. Bake at 350° for 18 to 20 minutes.

Mix powdered sugar and milk to make spreading consistency. Spread over slightly warm cookies. Cool; cut into bars. Makes 32.

Mincemeat Bars

       1 9-ounce package instant condensed
         mincemeat
       1 14-ounce can *sweetened*
         condensed milk
     ½ cup butter *or* margarine, softened
       1 cup packed brown sugar
       1 tablespoon milk
    1½ cups cornflakes, crushed (⅔ cup)
       1 cup all-purpose flour
       1 teaspoon baking soda

In saucepan crumble mincemeat; add sweetened condensed milk. Cook and stir till thickened, about 5 minutes; remove from heat.

Cream butter, brown sugar, and 1 tablespoon milk till fluffy. Stir cornflakes with flour and soda. Add to creamed mixture; mix well. Pat *half* of the crumb mixture into ungreased 13x9x2-inch baking pan. Carefully spread with mincemeat mixture. Sprinkle with remaining crumb mixture. Bake at 350° about 30 minutes. Cool; cut into bars. Makes 36.

Peanut-Chocolate Bars

     ½ cup shortening
     ½ cup granulated sugar
     ½ cup packed brown sugar
     ⅓ cup peanut butter
     ½ teaspoon vanilla
       1 egg
     ¼ cup milk
       1 cup all-purpose flour
     ½ teaspoon baking soda
     ½ teaspoon salt
       1 cup quick-cooking rolled oats
         Cocoa Fudge Frosting
         Butter Glaze

Cream together shortening, granulated sugar, brown sugar, peanut butter, and vanilla. Add egg and milk; beat well. Stir together flour, soda, and salt; add to creamed mixture. Beat just till well mixed. Stir in oats. Spread in greased 13x9x2-inch baking pan. Bake at 350° for 20 minutes. Cool. Prepare Cocoa Fudge Frosting; quickly spread over cookies. Drizzle with Butter Glaze; cut into bars. Makes 24.

Cocoa Fudge Frosting: Mix 2 cups sifted powdered sugar and ¼ cup unsweetened cocoa powder. Quickly stir in 3 tablespoons butter *or* margarine, melted; 2 to 3 tablespoons boiling water; and ½ teaspoon vanilla. Beat smooth.

Butter Glaze: Heat and stir 2 tablespoons butter *or* margarine over low heat till golden brown. Remove from heat; stir in 1 cup sifted powdered sugar and enough milk (3 to 4 teaspoons) to make of drizzling consistency.

TEST KITCHEN TIP

Crumbly toppings on cookies, such as *Mincemeat Bars*, add crunch and take the place of frosting. For streusel effect, sprinkle crumb mixture evenly over top.

Pecan Pie Bars

Well worth an occasional calorie splurge—

1½ **cups all-purpose flour**
  2 **tablespoons packed brown sugar**
 ½ **cup butter** *or* **margarine**
  2 **eggs**
 ½ **cup dark corn syrup**
 ½ **cup packed brown sugar**
 ½ **cup chopped pecans**
  2 **tablespoons butter, melted**
  1 **teaspoon vanilla**
 ¼ **teaspoon salt**

Mix flour and brown sugar; cut in butter. Pat into ungreased 11x7½x1½-inch baking pan. Bake at 350° for 15 minutes. Beat eggs slightly; stir in remaining ingredients. Pour over baked layer. Bake at 350° for 25 minutes. Cool till pecan layer is slightly firm before cutting into bars. Makes 32.

Apricot-Almond Bars

 ¾ **cup butter** *or* **margarine, softened**
 ½ **cup sifted powdered sugar**
 ¼ **teaspoon almond extract**
1¾ **cups all-purpose flour**
 ½ **cup finely chopped almonds**
 ¼ **teaspoon salt**
  1 **12-ounce jar apricot preserves**
 ½ **cup finely chopped candied fruits**
     and peels
 ½ **teaspoon almond extract**

Cream first 3 ingredients. Stir together flour, nuts, and salt; add to creamed mixture. Mix till crumbly. Reserve *1 cup* for topping; pat remaining into ungreased 13x9x2-inch baking pan. Combine preserves and remaining ingredients; spread over crumb layer. Top with reserved crumbs. Bake at 350° till golden, 30 to 35 minutes. Cut while warm. Makes 32.

◀ **When it's your turn** to serve refreshments, offer an assortment of bar cookies, such as *Candy-Meringue Bars* and *Fruit Cocktail Bars* (see recipe, page 23) on plate at left, chocolate-drizzled *Filbert Bars*, and *Apricot-Almond Bars.*

Candy-Meringue Bars

Meringue blankets a sweet layer of toffee candy—

 ½ **cup butter** *or* **margarine, softened**
  1 **cup packed brown sugar**
  2 **egg yolks**
  1 **teaspoon vanilla**
1½ **cups all-purpose flour**
 ¼ **teaspoon baking soda**
  2 **1⅛-ounce chocolate-coated**
     English toffee bars, chopped (½ cup)
  2 **egg whites**
 ½ **cup granulated sugar**

Cream butter and brown sugar; beat in yolks and vanilla. Stir together flour, soda, and ½ teaspoon salt. Add to creamed mixture; mix till crumbly. Pat into ungreased 13x9x2-inch baking pan. Sprinkle with toffee bars; press into base. Bake at 350° for 10 minutes. Beat whites till soft peaks form. Slowly add granulated sugar; beat to stiff peaks. Carefully spread over hot cookies. Bake 20 minutes longer. Cut into bars while warm. Makes 24.

Filbert Bars

Use either filberts, pecans, or black walnuts—

Stir together 2 cups all-purpose flour, ⅓ cup granulated sugar, 1 teaspoon baking powder, and ½ teaspoon salt. Cut in ¾ cup butter *or* margarine till crumbly. Combine 1 beaten egg yolk, 1 tablespoon water, and 1 teaspoon vanilla; mix into flour mixture. Pat *half* of dough into greased 13x9x2-inch baking pan. Mix 1 cup sifted powdered sugar; ⅔ cup finely chopped filberts, pecans, *or* black walnuts; 1 tablespoon orange liqueur *or* orange juice; and 1 egg white. Spread over dough in pan.

Between two sheets of waxed paper, roll remaining dough to 13x9-inch rectangle. Carefully peel off top paper. Invert dough and paper onto filling in pan; carefully remove paper. Pat dough to fit. Bake at 375° about 25 minutes. Cool; sift powdered sugar over top.

Melt together one 1-ounce square unsweetened chocolate and 1 tablespoon butter *or* margarine. Blend in ½ cup sifted powdered sugar and enough hot water to make of drizzling consistency. Drizzle over cooled cookies; let glaze set before cutting into bars. Makes 48.

TEST KITCHEN TIP

Slice jellied cranberry sauce crosswise, then cut each slice into small cubes for *Cran-Orange Bars*. Carefully fold cranberry into batter to avoid breaking cubes.

Hawaiian Fruit Bars

Light-textured, banana-flavored bar cookies pictured on pages 4 and 5 —

¼ **cup butter** *or* **margarine, softened**
½ **cup sugar**
½ **cup apricot, pineapple,** *or* **apricot-pineapple preserves**
1 **egg**
½ **teaspoon vanilla**
• • •
⅔ **cup all-purpose flour**
¼ **teaspoon baking powder**
¼ **teaspoon baking soda**
⅛ **teaspoon salt**
1 **ripe small banana, mashed (¼ cup)**
½ **cup flaked coconut**
• • •
½ **cup apricot, pineapple,** *or* **apricot-pineapple preserves**
¼ **cup chopped almonds**

In mixing bowl cream together the butter or margarine and sugar till fluffy. Add the ½ cup preserves, egg, and vanilla to the creamed mixture; mix well.

Thoroughly stir together the flour, baking powder, baking soda, and salt. Stir into creamed mixture. Blend in the mashed banana and coconut; mix well. Spread in greased 9x9x2-inch baking pan. Bake at 350° till cookies test done, 23 to 25 minutes. Spread warm cookies with the remaining ½ cup preserves. Sprinkle with the chopped almonds. Cool cookies thoroughly; cut into bars. Makes 24.

Cran-Orange Bars

See footnote on page 25 for toasting nuts —

6 **tablespoons butter** *or* **margarine, softened**
¾ **cup granulated sugar**
¾ **cup orange marmalade**
2 **eggs**
1½ **cups all-purpose flour**
1 **teaspoon baking powder**
¾ **teaspoon salt**
1 **8-ounce can jellied cranberry sauce**
• • •
1 **cup sifted powdered sugar**
2 **tablespoons butter** *or* **margarine, melted**
Milk
¼ **cup finely chopped pecans, toasted**

Cream softened butter with granulated sugar. Add marmalade and eggs; mix well. Stir together flour, baking powder, and salt; add to creamed mixture. Stir just till moistened. Cut cranberry sauce into ¼-inch cubes; reserve 2 tablespoons. Gently fold remaining cubes into batter. Spread in greased 13x9x2-inch baking pan. Bake at 350° for 30 to 35 minutes.

Combine powdered sugar, melted butter, and reserved cranberry; add enough milk (2 to 3 teaspoons) to make of spreading consistency. Spread over warm cookies; top with nuts. Cool; cut into bars. Refrigerate. Makes 36.

Custard Bars

Cream ½ cup softened butter *or* margarine and ½ cup packed brown sugar. Stir together 1⅓ cups all-purpose flour, ½ teaspoon ground cinnamon, ½ teaspoon ground ginger, ¼ teaspoon salt, and ¼ teaspoon ground nutmeg. Add to creamed mixture; beat on low speed of electric mixer just till blended. Reserve ½ cup; pat remaining dough into greased 9x9x2-inch baking pan. Bake at 350° for 15 minutes.

Mix 1 cup dairy sour cream, 1 egg, ¼ cup granulated sugar, ½ teaspoon baking soda, and dash salt; beat smooth. Spread over baked layer. Toss ⅓ cup chopped nuts with reserved crumb mixture; sprinkle over cream layer. Bake at 350° for 12 to 15 minutes. Cut into bars while warm. Store in refrigerator. Makes 24.

Almond-Coconut Bars

Good for gift giving as shown on pages 82 and 83 —

  1 cup all-purpose flour
  ½ cup sifted powdered sugar
  ½ cup shredded coconut
  ½ teaspoon salt
  ½ cup butter *or* margarine
      • • •
  ½ cup semisweet chocolate pieces
  1 package coconut-almond frosting mix
      (for 2-layer cake)
  ½ cup chopped almonds

Stir together flour, powdered sugar, coconut, and salt. Cut in butter till crumbly. Pat into ungreased 13x9x2-inch baking pan. Bake at 375° for 10 to 12 minutes. Immediately top with chocolate pieces; spread when soft. Prepare frosting mix following package directions. Stir in almonds; carefully spread over chocolate layer. Bake at 375° till golden, about 18 minutes. Cool; cut into bars. Makes 48.

Cheesecake Bars

A tangy bar cookie shown on pages 4 and 5 —

  ⅔ cup finely crushed graham crackers
      (9 square crackers)
  ½ cup all-purpose flour
  ½ cup chopped nuts
  ¼ cup sugar
  ½ cup butter *or* margarine, melted
  1 8-ounce package cream cheese,
      softened
  ⅓ cup sugar
  1 egg
  ½ teaspoon grated lemon peel
  1 tablespoon lemon juice
  2 tablespoons finely crushed graham
      crackers

Stir together first 4 ingredients. Add melted butter; mix till crumbly. Pat into ungreased 9x9x2-inch baking pan. Bake at 350° for 12 minutes. Cream together cream cheese and ⅓ cup sugar. Add egg, lemon peel, and lemon juice; mix well. Pour over baked layer. Bake at 350° for 20 to 25 minutes. Sprinkle with the 2 tablespoons graham crackers. Cool; cut into bars. Store in refrigerator. Makes 36.

Eggnog Bars

  ½ cup butter *or* margarine, softened
  1 cup granulated sugar
  1½ teaspoons brandy *or* rum flavoring
  2¼ cups all-purpose flour
  1 teaspoon baking soda
  ¼ teaspoon ground nutmeg
  1 cup dairy *or* canned eggnog
  1 cup chopped candied cherries
  ½ cup chopped almonds
  ¾ cup sifted powdered sugar
  Milk

Cream first 2 ingredients; blend in *1 teaspoon* flavoring. Stir flour with soda, nutmeg, and ¼ teaspoon salt. Add alternately with eggnog to creamed mixture. Stir in cherries and nuts. Spread in greased 15½x10½x1-inch baking pan. Bake at 350° for 18 to 20 minutes. Mix powdered sugar, remaining ½ teaspoon flavoring, and enough milk (3 to 4 teaspoons) to make mixture pourable. Drizzle over warm cookies. Cool; cut into bars. Makes 48.

Fruit Cocktail Bars

Excellent served with punch as shown on page 20 —

  1 8-ounce can fruit cocktail
  ¼ cup butter *or* margarine, softened
  ⅓ cup sugar
  1 egg
  ¼ teaspoon vanilla
  1¼ cups all-purpose flour
  ¼ teaspoon baking powder
  ¼ teaspoon baking soda
  1 tablespoon red maraschino cherry
      syrup
  ½ cup flaked coconut
  ¼ cup chopped red maraschino cherries

Drain fruit; reserve ⅓ cup syrup. Chop fruit; set aside. Cream butter and sugar; beat in egg and vanilla. Stir flour with baking powder, soda, and ¼ teaspoon salt. Mix reserved syrup with cherry syrup. Add flour mixture alternately with syrups to creamed mixture; mix well. Stir in fruit, coconut, and cherries. Spread in greased 9x9x2-inch baking pan. Bake at 350° for 30 to 35 minutes. Cool. If desired, sift powdered sugar over top. Cut. Makes 24.

Frosted Pecan Bars

Nut-topped bars shown on pages 82 and 83 —

> 6 tablespoons butter *or* margarine,
>   softened
> 1 cup packed brown sugar
> 2 eggs
> ¼ cup milk
> ½ teaspoon vanilla
> ½ teaspoon maple flavoring
> 1 cup all-purpose flour
> 1 teaspoon baking powder
> ¼ teaspoon salt
> ¾ cup chopped pecans
>   Maple Frosting

Cream together butter or margarine and brown sugar till light and fluffy. Add eggs; beat well. Blend in milk, vanilla, and maple flavoring. Thoroughly stir together flour, baking powder, and salt; stir into creamed mixture. Stir in ½ *cup* of the chopped pecans. Pour batter into greased 13x9x2-inch baking pan. Bake at 350° till done, about 25 minutes. Cool; spread with Maple Frosting. Top with remaining chopped nuts. Cut into bars. Makes 48.

Maple Frosting: Cream ¼ cup softened butter; gradually add 2 cups sifted powdered sugar. Stir in ¼ teaspoon maple flavoring and enough milk till of spreading consistency.

Glazed Walnut Bars

Lemon topper complements this sweet, nutty bar —

In bowl thoroughly stir together 1 cup all-purpose flour, ¼ cup granulated sugar, and ¼ teaspoon salt; cut in 6 tablespoons butter *or* margarine till mixture is crumbly. Firmly pat mixture into ungreased 9x9x2-inch baking pan. Bake at 350° for 12 to 15 minutes.

Thoroughly stir together 1 cup packed brown sugar, 2 tablespoons all-purpose flour, ¼ teaspoon baking powder, and ¼ teaspoon salt. Add 2 slightly beaten eggs and 1½ teaspoons vanilla; mix well. Stir in 1 cup chopped walnuts. Spread over baked layer. Bake at 350° for 25 minutes. Spread with Lemon Glaze while warm. Cool; cut into bars. Makes 24.

Lemon Glaze: Combine ½ cup sifted powdered sugar; 1 tablespoon butter, melted; and 2 teaspoons lemon juice. Beat till smooth.

Velvet Pistachio Squares

> ½ cup butter *or* margarine, softened
> ½ cup sugar
> 1 egg
> 1 teaspoon vanilla
> 1 cup all-purpose flour
> ½ teaspoon baking powder
> ½ cup milk
> ⅓ cup flaked coconut
> 6 tablespoons chopped pistachio nuts
>   Vanilla Frosting

Cream butter and sugar; blend in egg and vanilla. Stir together flour, baking powder, and ¼ teaspoon salt; add alternately with milk to creamed mixture. Mix well. Stir in coconut and *4 tablespoons* of the nuts. Spread in greased 9x9x2-inch baking pan. Bake at 350° for 20 minutes. Cool. Spread with Vanilla Frosting; top with remaining nuts. Cut into squares. Makes 36.

Vanilla Frosting: Mix 1 cup sifted powdered sugar, 2 tablespoons softened butter *or* margarine, and ¼ teaspoon vanilla. Add milk (2 to 3 teaspoons) till of spreading consistency.

Blarney Stone Bars

> 3 egg yolks
> 1 cup sugar
> 1 teaspoon vanilla
> 1 cup all-purpose flour
> 1 teaspoon baking powder
> 4 stiffly beaten egg whites
>   Sweet Butter Icing
> 1 cup finely chopped peanuts

In large bowl beat egg yolks; add sugar and vanilla. Beat till thick and lemon-colored. Stir together flour and baking powder; stir into yolk mixture. Add ½ cup boiling water; mix well. Fold in egg whites. Spread in greased 15½x10½x1-inch baking pan. Bake at 350° till done, about 20 minutes. Cool; frost with Sweet Butter Icing. Top with nuts, lightly pressing into frosting. Cut into bars. Makes 36.

Sweet Butter Icing: In small bowl combine 2 cups sifted powdered sugar; 6 tablespoons butter *or* margarine, melted; and 1 egg yolk. Beat smooth. Add enough milk (about 1 tablespoon) till of spreading consistency.

Danish Pastry Apple Bars

    2½ cups all-purpose flour
    1 cup shortening
    1 egg yolk
      Milk
    1 cup cornflakes
    8 to 10 tart apples, peeled, cored, and
      sliced (8 cups)
    ¾ to 1 cup granulated sugar
    1 teaspoon ground cinnamon
    1 egg white
    1 cup sifted powdered sugar
    3 to 4 teaspoons milk

Stir together flour and 1 teaspoon salt; cut in shortening. In measuring cup beat egg yolk; add enough milk to measure ⅔ cup. Mix well; stir into flour mixture. On floured surface roll *half* of the dough to 17x12-inch rectangle; fit into bottom and up sides of 15½x10½x1-inch baking pan. Sprinkle with cornflakes; top with apple slices. Mix granulated sugar and cinnamon; sprinkle over apples. Roll remaining dough to 15½x10½-inch rectangle; place over apples. Seal edges; cut slits in top.

Beat egg white till frothy; brush on top. Bake at 375° for 50 minutes. While warm, drizzle with mixture of powdered sugar and 3 to 4 teaspoons milk. Cool; cut into bars. Makes 36.

Stuffed Date Bars

A pecan-stuffed date is in each bar—

Slit 30 whole pitted dates (about 8 ounces). Using 30 small pecan halves, stuff dates with nuts; set aside. In saucepan melt ¼ cup butter. Stir in 1 cup packed brown sugar till well blended. Remove from heat; cool to lukewarm. Blend in ½ cup dairy sour cream, 2 beaten eggs, and 1 teaspoon vanilla; mix thoroughly.

Stir together 1 cup all-purpose flour, ¼ teaspoon baking powder, ¼ teaspoon baking soda, ¼ teaspoon salt, and ¼ teaspoon ground ginger. Add to sour cream mixture; mix well.

Pour into greased 13x9x2-inch baking pan. Carefully arrange stuffed dates atop batter in 5 lengthwise rows with 6 stuffed dates in each row. Bake at 350° for 25 to 30 minutes. Cool; cut into bars, allowing 1 date per bar. Sift powdered sugar over top. Makes 30.

Viennese Almond Bars

Colorful and appealing for a holiday tea—

    ½ cup butter *or* margarine, softened
    ½ cup packed brown sugar
    2 tablespoons milk
    1½ cups all-purpose flour
    ⅓ cup raspberry preserves *or* jam
          • • •
    ½ cup granulated sugar
    1 tablespoon all-purpose flour
    ¼ cup milk
    2 tablespoons butter *or* margarine
    ¾ cup chopped almonds, toasted*
          • • •
    ¼ cup milk chocolate pieces *or*
      semisweet chocolate pieces

Cream ½ cup butter and brown sugar till fluffy; beat in 2 tablespoons milk. Blend in 1½ cups flour till crumbly. Pat mixture into ungreased 9x9x2-inch baking pan. Spread raspberry preserves or jam over cookie base.

In small saucepan combine granulated sugar and 1 tablespoon flour; stir in ¼ cup milk and 2 tablespoons butter or margarine. Bring to a boil; cook and stir 2 minutes. Remove from heat; stir in the toasted almonds.

Carefully spoon hot mixture over preserves. Bake at 375° till golden and bubbly all over, about 25 minutes. Immediately sprinkle chocolate pieces over top; when soft, spread lightly over top. Cool; cut into bars. Makes 36.

*To toast nuts, spread on baking sheet. Heat at 375° about 5 minutes; stir occasionally.

TEST KITCHEN TIP

To prepare dates for *Stuffed Date Bars*, slit each date and fill with a pecan half. Arrange in rows atop batter. After baking, cut into bars between rows of dates.

Show-Off Brownies

German Chocolate Brownies

Shown on pages 82 and 83—

1 4-ounce package sweet cooking
   chocolate
6 tablespoons butter *or* margarine
2 beaten eggs
¼ cup sugar
2 tablespoons milk
1 teaspoon vanilla
½ cup all-purpose flour
½ teaspoon baking powder
   Coconut Topper

In saucepan melt chocolate and butter; stir constantly. Remove from heat. Add eggs, sugar, milk, and vanilla; mix well. Stir together flour and baking powder; stir into chocolate mixture. Spread in greased 9x9x2-inch baking pan. Bake at 350° for 15 minutes. Spread with Coconut Topper; bake at 350° for 25 to 30 minutes more. Cool; cut into bars. Makes 20.

Coconut Topper: In medium mixing bowl beat 2 egg yolks with ⅔ cup sugar; one 5⅓-ounce can evaporated milk (⅔ cup); and ¼ cup butter *or* margarine, melted. Stir in 1 cup flaked coconut and ½ cup chopped walnuts.

Butterscotch Fudge Bars

A favorite with our taste panel—

In saucepan melt ½ cup butter *or* margarine and one 1-ounce square unsweetened chocolate; remove from heat. Stir in 1½ cups packed brown sugar. Add 3 eggs; beat just till blended. Stir in 1 teaspoon vanilla. Stir together 1½ cups all-purpose flour and ½ teaspoon baking soda; stir into batter. Fold in ½ cup chopped nuts. Spread in greased 9x9x2-inch baking pan. Bake at 350° for 30 to 35 minutes. Cool; top with Golden Frosting. Cut into bars. Makes 36.

Golden Frosting: Lightly brown 6 tablespoons butter *or* margarine; cool. Gradually beat in 2 cups sifted powdered sugar and ½ teaspoon vanilla. Slowly add hot water (about 2 tablespoons) till of spreading consistency.

Tri-Level Brownies

1 cup quick-cooking rolled oats
½ cup all-purpose flour
½ cup packed brown sugar
¼ teaspoon baking soda
6 tablespoons butter *or* margarine,
   melted
¾ cup granulated sugar
¼ cup butter *or* margarine, melted
1 1-ounce square unsweetened
   chocolate, melted and cooled
1 egg
⅔ cup all-purpose flour
¼ teaspoon baking powder
¼ cup milk
½ teaspoon vanilla
½ cup chopped walnuts
   Fudge Frosting

For bottom layer, stir together first 4 ingredients and ¼ teaspoon salt. Stir in 6 tablespoons melted butter. Pat in 11x7½x1½-inch baking pan. Bake at 350° for 10 minutes.

For middle layer, combine granulated sugar, ¼ cup butter, and chocolate; add egg. Beat well. Stir together ⅔ cup flour, baking powder, and ¼ teaspoon salt; add to chocolate mixture alternately with a mixture of the milk and vanilla, mixing after each addition. Fold in nuts. Spread batter over baked layer. Continue baking at 350° for 25 minutes. Cool. Frost with Fudge Frosting. Cut into bars. Top with walnut halves, if desired. Makes 16.

Fudge Frosting: In small saucepan melt one 1-ounce square unsweetened chocolate and 2 tablespoons butter *or* margarine over low heat; stir constantly. Remove from heat; stir in 1½ cups sifted powdered sugar and 1 teaspoon vanilla. Blend in hot water (about 2 tablespoons) to make almost pourable consistency.

Tempting *Tri-Level Brownies* boast a nut-rich chocolate layer sandwiched between a crunchy oatmeal base and a smooth fudge frosting. ▶

TEST KITCHEN TIP

For marbled brownies, spoon dark batter in checkerboard fashion into pan and fill open spaces with light batter. Then, lightly swirl batters together with spatula.

Marble Fudge Brownies

See footnote on page 25 for toasting nuts—

  ¾ cup shortening
  1 cup sugar
  3 eggs
  1 teaspoon vanilla
  1 cup all-purpose flour
  ¾ teaspoon baking powder
  ¼ teaspoon salt
    • • •
  1 tablespoon instant coffee crystals
  1 tablespoon water
  2 1-ounce squares unsweetened
      chocolate, melted and cooled
    • • •
  ½ cup milk chocolate pieces
  ¼ cup finely chopped almonds, toasted

Cream shortening and sugar till fluffy; beat in eggs just till blended. Mix in vanilla. Stir together flour, baking powder, and salt; stir into creamed mixture. Spoon *half* of the batter into another bowl. Dissolve coffee crystals in the water; stir coffee and melted chocolate into remaining batter. Drop chocolate mixture from tablespoon checkerboard fashion into greased 13x9x2-inch baking pan. (See picture above.) Fill in spaces with light batter.

Swirl with spatula to marble; do not overmix. Bake at 350° for 22 to 25 minutes. Immediately sprinkle milk chocolate pieces over top. Let stand 2 to 3 minutes to melt; spread chocolate evenly over brownies. Sprinkle with almonds. Cool; cut into bars. Makes 32.

Mint Swirl Brownies

Colorful brownies shown on pages 4 and 5—

  1 3-ounce package cream cheese,
      softened
  ¼ cup butter *or* margarine, softened
  ¾ cup sugar
  2 eggs
  ⅔ cup all-purpose flour
  ½ teaspoon baking powder
  ¼ teaspoon salt
    • • •
  ⅓ cup chopped nuts
  1 1-ounce square unsweetened
      chocolate, melted and cooled
    • • •
  ½ teaspoon peppermint extract
    Several drops green food coloring
    Chocolate Glaze

Cream together cream cheese, butter, and sugar; beat in eggs. Stir together flour, baking powder, and salt; stir into creamed mixture.

Spoon *half* of the batter into another bowl; stir in nuts and chocolate. Drop chocolate batter from tablespoon checkerboard fashion into greased 9x9x2-inch baking pan. (See picture at left.) To remaining batter, stir in extract and food coloring. Spoon green batter into open spaces in baking pan. Swirl with spatula to marble; do not overmix. Bake at 350° for 15 to 20 minutes. Cool; pour Chocolate Glaze over top. Cut into bars. Makes 24.

Chocolate Glaze: Melt one 1-ounce square unsweetened chocolate and 1 tablespoon butter *or* margarine over low heat; stir constantly. Remove from heat; stir in 1 cup sifted powdered sugar and ½ teaspoon vanilla till crumbly. Blend in enough boiling water (about 2 tablespoons) till of pouring consistency.

Saucepan Fudge Brownies

In saucepan melt ½ cup butter *or* margarine and two 1-ounce squares unsweetened chocolate. Remove from heat; stir in 1 cup sugar. Blend in 2 eggs, one at a time. Add 1 teaspoon vanilla. Stir in ¾ cup all-purpose flour and ½ cup chopped nuts; mix well. Spread in greased 8x8x2-inch baking pan. Bake at 350° for 30 minutes. Cool; cut into squares. Makes 16.

Buttermilk Brownies

A large recipe to serve a crowd—

1 cup butter *or* margarine
⅓ cup unsweetened cocoa powder
2 cups all-purpose flour
2 cups sugar
1 teaspoon baking soda
½ teaspoon salt
2 slightly beaten eggs
½ cup buttermilk
1½ teaspoons vanilla
    Cocoa-Buttermilk Frosting

In saucepan combine butter, cocoa, and 1 cup water. Bring to boil; stir constantly. Remove from heat. In large mixing bowl stir together flour, sugar, soda, and salt; stir in eggs, buttermilk, and vanilla. Add cocoa mixture; mix till blended. Pour into *one* greased 15½x10½x1-inch baking pan, *or two* 11x7½x1½-inch baking pans, *or two* 9x9x2-inch baking pans. Bake at 375° for 20 minutes. Immediately pour Cocoa-Buttermilk Frosting over brownies; spread evenly. Cool; cut into bars. Makes 60.

Cocoa-Buttermilk Frosting: In saucepan mix ¼ cup butter, 3 tablespoons unsweetened cocoa powder, and 3 tablespoons buttermilk. Cook and stir to boiling; remove from heat. Beat in 2¼ cups sifted powdered sugar, ½ cup chopped walnuts, and ½ teaspoon vanilla.

Pound Cake Brownies

¾ cup butter *or* margarine, softened
1 cup sugar
3 eggs
2 1-ounce squares unsweetened
    chocolate, melted and cooled
1 teaspoon vanilla
1¼ cups all-purpose flour
½ teaspoon baking powder
½ cup chopped nuts

Cream butter and sugar; beat in eggs. Blend in chocolate and vanilla. Stir flour with baking powder and ¼ teaspoon salt. Add to creamed mixture; mix well. Stir in nuts. Spread in greased 9x9x2-inch baking pan. Bake at 350° for 25 to 30 minutes. Cool. If desired, sift powdered sugar over top. Cut into bars. Makes 24.

Cheese-Marbled Brownies

1 6-ounce package semisweet chocolate
    pieces (1 cup)
6 tablespoons butter *or* margarine
⅓ cup honey
2 beaten eggs
1 teaspoon vanilla
    • • •
½ cup all-purpose flour
½ teaspoon baking powder
    Cheese Filling

Melt chocolate and butter over low heat; stir constantly. Cool. Gradually add honey to eggs. Blend in chocolate mixture and vanilla. Stir together flour and baking powder. Add to chocolate mixture; stir just till dry ingredients are moistened. Pour *half* of the batter into greased 9x9x2-inch baking pan. Bake at 350° for 10 minutes. Pour Cheese Filling over partially baked layer. Carefully spoon remaining brownie batter over filling; swirl slightly with cheese. Bake at 350° for 30 to 35 minutes. Cool; cut into bars. Makes 24.

Cheese Filling: In mixing bowl cream together one 8-ounce package softened cream cheese and ½ cup sugar; beat in 1 egg and dash salt. Stir in ½ cup chopped nuts.

Semisweet Frosted Brownies

Cream ¾ cup softened butter *or* margarine and 2 cups sugar; add 4 eggs, one at a time, beating well after each. Blend in four 1-ounce squares unsweetened chocolate, melted and cooled, and 1 teaspoon vanilla.

Stir together 1⅔ cups all-purpose flour, 1 teaspoon baking powder, and ½ teaspoon salt. Stir into chocolate mixture. Stir in 1 cup chopped walnuts. Spread in greased 15½x10½x1-inch baking pan. Bake at 350° for 20 to 25 minutes. Cool. Frost with Semisweet Chocolate Frosting; cut into bars. Makes 60.

Semisweet Chocolate Frosting: In small saucepan melt ½ cup semisweet chocolate pieces and 2 tablespoons butter *or* margarine over low heat, stirring constantly. Remove from heat; beat in 1 cup sifted powdered sugar. Add enough milk (about 3 tablespoons) till frosting is of spreading consistency.

Brownie Mix

5 cups sugar
3 cups all-purpose flour
2 cups unsweetened cocoa powder
3 teaspoons baking powder
3 teaspoons salt
3½ cups shortening that does not
   require refrigeration

In large bowl thoroughly stir together first 5 ingredients. Cut in shortening till mixture resembles coarse cornmeal. Store in covered container up to 6 weeks at room temperature. For longer storage, place in freezer. To measure, lightly spoon mix into measuring cup; level with spatula. Makes about 14 cups or enough for 5 single recipes of Brownies.

To make Brownies: Beat 2 eggs with 1 teaspoon vanilla. Add 2¾ cups Brownie Mix; stir till nearly smooth. If desired, stir in ½ cup chopped nuts, *or* semisweet chocolate pieces, *or* butterscotch pieces. Spread in greased 8x8x 2-inch baking pan. Bake at 350° for 25 to 30 minutes. Cool; cut into squares. Makes 16.

For 35 thinner brownies, double recipe. Bake in greased 15½x10½x1-inch baking pan.

Raisin-Oatmeal Brownies

¾ cup quick-cooking rolled oats
1 6-ounce package semisweet chocolate
   pieces (1 cup)
6 tablespoons butter *or* margarine
½ cup packed brown sugar
2 eggs
1 teaspoon vanilla
¾ cup all-purpose flour
½ cup raisins
¼ teaspoon baking soda
¼ teaspoon salt

Sprinkle *2 tablespoons* of the oats over bottom of greased 9x9x2-inch baking pan; set aside. In saucepan melt chocolate and butter over low heat; stir constantly. Remove from heat; blend in sugar. Beat in eggs and vanilla. Stir together flour, remaining oats, raisins, soda, and salt; stir into chocolate mixture. Spoon into prepared pan. Bake at 325° about 30 minutes. Cool; cut into bars. Makes 24.

Chocolate Pudding Brownies

6 tablespoons butter *or* margarine,
   softened
⅔ cup granulated sugar
2 eggs
¼ cup milk
1 teaspoon vanilla
½ cup all-purpose flour
1 3¾- or 4-ounce package *regular*
   chocolate pudding mix
½ teaspoon baking powder
¼ teaspoon salt
½ cup chopped nuts
   Powdered sugar

Cream butter and granulated sugar. Blend in eggs, milk, and vanilla. Stir together flour, pudding mix, baking powder, and salt. Add to creamed mixture; mix well. Stir in nuts. Spread in greased 9x9x2-inch baking pan. Bake at 350° for 25 to 30 minutes. Cool. Sift powdered sugar over top. Cut into bars. Makes 24.

Fudgy Granola Brownies

¾ cup butter *or* margarine
2 1-ounce squares unsweetened
   chocolate
1½ cups sugar
3 eggs
1 cup all-purpose flour
1 teaspoon baking powder
½ teaspoon salt
1 cup granola cereal
   Chocolate Frosting

In medium saucepan melt butter or margarine with chocolate; remove from heat. Stir in sugar, then eggs. Stir together flour, baking powder, and salt. Add to chocolate mixture; beat well. Stir in granola cereal. Spread in greased 13x9x2-inch baking pan. Bake at 350° for 25 to 30 minutes. Cool. Top with Chocolate Frosting. Cut into bars. Makes 32.

Chocolate Frosting: In small saucepan heat together 2 tablespoons butter *or* margarine, 2 tablespoons milk, and one 1-ounce square unsweetened chocolate; remove from heat. Stir in 1 cup sifted powdered sugar. If necessary, thin with a little additional milk.

Crackle Brownies

Serve the same day as baked to retain crispness—

1 5¾-ounce package milk chocolate
   pieces (1 cup)
⅓ cup butter *or* margarine, softened
¾ cup sugar
2 eggs
1 teaspoon vanilla
1 cup all-purpose flour
½ teaspoon baking powder
⅓ cup crisp rice cereal

Melt ½ *cup* of the chocolate over low heat; cool. Cream butter and sugar; beat in eggs just till blended. Stir in cooled chocolate and vanilla. Stir together flour, baking powder, and ¼ teaspoon salt; add to chocolate mixture. Mix well. Spread in greased 9x9x2-inch baking pan. Bake at 350° for 25 to 30 minutes. Immediately sprinkle with remaining chocolate; let stand 5 minutes. Spread evenly over top; sprinkle with cereal. Cool; cut into bars. Makes 24.

Spice Brownies

½ cup shortening
1 cup packed brown sugar
2 eggs
¼ cup milk
1 teaspoon vanilla
⅔ cup all-purpose flour
⅓ cup unsweetened cocoa powder
½ teaspoon baking powder
½ teaspoon ground cinnamon
¼ teaspoon ground ginger
½ cup chopped nuts
  Spice Frosting

Cream shortening and sugar till fluffy; beat in eggs, milk, and vanilla. Stir together flour, cocoa, baking powder, spices, and ¼ teaspoon salt; blend into creamed mixture. Stir in nuts. Spread in greased 9x9x2-inch baking pan. Bake at 350° for 20 to 25 minutes. Cool. Frost with Spice Frosting. Cut. Makes 20.

Spice Frosting: Stir together 1 cup sifted powdered sugar and ⅛ teaspoon ground cinnamon. Cream 2 tablespoons softened butter *or* margarine with sugar. Add enough milk (1 to 2 tablespoons) till of spreading consistency.

Rocky Road Brownies

Marshmallow layer cuts easily with wet knife—

6 tablespoons butter *or* margarine
1 1-ounce square unsweetened
   chocolate
1 cup sugar
1 teaspoon vanilla
2 eggs
¾ cup all-purpose flour
½ teaspoon salt
½ teaspoon baking powder
½ cup chopped pecans
26 large marshmallows, halved
   Chocolate Glaze (see recipe,
   page 28)

In saucepan melt butter and chocolate over low heat; stir constantly. Remove from heat. Add sugar and vanilla; mix well. Beat in eggs. Stir together flour, salt, and baking powder; add to chocolate mixture, blending well. Stir in nuts. Spread in greased 11x7½x1½-inch baking pan. Bake at 350° for 20 to 25 minutes.

When done, immediately arrange marshmallow halves over top, 6 rows crosswise and 9 rows lengthwise. Return to oven 2 to 3 minutes. While hot, drizzle with Chocolate Glaze. Cool. Use a wet knife to cut into bars. Makes 24.

Chocolate Syrup Brownies

½ cup butter *or* margarine, softened
1 cup sugar
4 eggs
1 16-ounce can chocolate-flavored
   syrup (1½ cups)
1¼ cups all-purpose flour
1 cup chopped walnuts
  Quick Frosting

Cream butter and sugar; beat in eggs. Blend in syrup and flour; stir in nuts. Pour into greased 13x9x2-inch baking pan. Bake at 350° for 30 to 35 minutes. Cool slightly; top with Quick Frosting. Cool; cut into bars. Makes 32.

Quick Frosting: Mix ⅔ cup sugar, 3 tablespoons milk, and 3 tablespoons butter *or* margarine. Bring to boil; boil 30 seconds. Remove from heat; stir in ½ cup semisweet chocolate pieces till melted. Mixture will be thin.

Date Layer Brownies

Date Filling
¾ cup shortening
2 1-ounce squares unsweetened
   chocolate
1 cup packed brown sugar
2 eggs
1 teaspoon vanilla
1⅓ cups all-purpose flour
1 teaspoon baking powder
½ teaspoon salt
⅓ cup chopped nuts

Prepare Date Filling; cool. In medium saucepan melt shortening and chocolate over low heat; remove from heat. Stir in sugar; blend in eggs and vanilla. Stir together flour, baking powder, and salt; add to chocolate batter. Mix well. Spread *half* of the batter in greased 9x9x 2-inch baking pan. Spoon filling over; spread carefully. Spread remaining batter over filling. Top with nuts. Bake at 350° for 30 to 35 minutes. Cool; cut into bars. Makes 24.

Date Filling: In small saucepan combine ¾ cup finely chopped pitted dates (4 ounces), ½ cup water, ¼ cup granulated sugar, and ⅛ teaspoon salt. Cook and stir over low heat till thickened, 3 to 4 minutes. Remove from heat; stir in ¼ teaspoon vanilla.

Sugar Brownies

In saucepan combine one 4-ounce package sweet cooking chocolate, broken up, and 2 tablespoons butter *or* margarine. Melt over low heat, stirring constantly. Remove from heat; stir in ¾ cup sugar and 1 teaspoon vanilla. Beat in 2 eggs. Stir together ½ cup all-purpose flour, ½ teaspoon baking powder, and ¼ teaspoon salt; add to chocolate mixture. Blend well. Stir in ½ cup chopped walnuts.

Slice 1 roll refrigerated sugar cookie dough (8 ounces) into ⅛-inch-thick slices. Arrange *half* of the slices in bottom of ungreased 13x9x 2-inch baking pan; pat to cover bottom of pan. Spread *half* of the chocolate batter over cookie layer. Top with remaining sliced cookies. Carefully spread remaining batter over all. Bake at 350° for 25 to 30 minutes. Cool; cut into bars. Makes 36.

Peanut Butter Brownies

¼ cup shortening
2 1-ounce squares unsweetened
   chocolate
1 cup sugar
¼ cup peanut butter
2 eggs
½ teaspoon vanilla
½ cup all-purpose flour
¼ teaspoon baking soda
½ of a 16-ounce can ready-to-spread
   chocolate frosting (about 1 cup)
2 tablespoons peanut butter
3 tablespoons chopped peanuts

Melt shortening with chocolate; remove from heat. Blend in sugar and ¼ cup peanut butter. Add eggs and vanilla; beat smooth. Stir together flour, soda, and ¼ teaspoon salt; stir into batter. Spread in greased 9x9x2-inch baking pan. Bake at 350° for 20 minutes; cool. Mix frosting and 2 tablespoons peanut butter; spread on cookies. Top with chopped nuts; cut into bars. Makes 24.

Marmalade Brownies

1 cup sugar
⅓ cup unsweetened cocoa powder
6 tablespoons butter, melted
2 eggs
¼ cup orange marmalade
½ teaspoon vanilla
1 cup all-purpose flour
½ teaspoon baking powder
⅓ cup chopped pecans
Marmalade Glaze

Combine sugar and cocoa; stir in butter, eggs, marmalade, and vanilla. Stir together flour, baking powder, and ¼ teaspoon salt; stir into cocoa mixture. Mix in nuts. Spread in greased 9x9x2-inch baking pan. Bake at 350° for 30 minutes. Top warm brownies with Marmalade Glaze. Cool; cut into bars. Makes 24.

Marmalade Glaze: Blend together ½ cup sifted powdered sugar, 3 tablespoons marmalade (cut up large pieces of peel), and 2 tablespoons softened butter *or* margarine. Add enough milk till of spreading consistency.

Marshmallow Brownies

Marshmallows disappear to add sweetness—

    1½ cups tiny marshmallows
    1 6-ounce package semisweet chocolate
        pieces (1 cup)
    ½ cup butter *or* margarine
    2 eggs
    1 teaspoon vanilla
    ½ cup all-purpose flour
    ¼ teaspoon baking powder
        Dash salt
    ½ cup chopped walnuts
        Marshmallow Frosting

In saucepan combine marshmallows, chocolate, and butter; melt over low heat, stirring constantly. Cool. Blend in eggs and vanilla.

Thoroughly stir together flour, baking powder, and salt; blend into chocolate mixture. Stir in chopped nuts. Spread in greased 9x9x2-inch baking pan. Bake at 350° for 15 to 20 minutes. Cool. Frost brownies with Marshmallow Frosting. Cut into bars. Makes 20.

Marshmallow Frosting: In saucepan combine ½ cup tiny marshmallows, ½ of a 1-ounce square unsweetened chocolate, 1 tablespoon butter *or* margarine, and 4 teaspoons milk. Melt over low heat, stirring constantly. Remove from heat; beat in ¾ cup sifted powdered sugar.

Brandy Alexander Brownies

Reminds you of the popular after-dinner drink—

Cream 6 tablespoons softened butter *or* margarine with ¾ cup sugar till fluffy. Add 2 eggs; beat well. Blend in one 1-ounce square unsweetened chocolate, melted and cooled; 2 tablespoons dark crème de cacao; and 2 tablespoons brandy. Stir together ⅔ cup all-purpose flour, ½ teaspoon baking powder, and ¼ teaspoon salt. Stir into creamed mixture. Stir in ⅓ cup chopped nuts. Spread in greased 9x9x2-inch baking pan. Bake at 350° for 20 to 25 minutes. Cool. Frost with Sweet Brandy Frosting. Cut into bars. Makes 24.

Sweet Brandy Frosting: Cream together 2 tablespoons softened butter *or* margarine and 1 cup sifted powdered sugar. Blend in 1 tablespoon dark crème de cacao and 1 tablespoon brandy to make of spreading consistency.

Mocha Brownies

An excellent partner for afternoon coffee—

In saucepan melt ½ cup butter *or* margarine; remove from heat. Blend in ⅔ cup sugar. Add 2 eggs; beat well. Stir in 1 teaspoon vanilla. Stir together ½ cup all-purpose flour, 3 tablespoons unsweetened cocoa powder, 1 tablespoon instant coffee crystals, ½ teaspoon baking powder, and ¼ teaspoon salt. Stir into egg mixture. Mix in ½ cup chopped nuts. Spread batter in greased 8x8x2-inch baking pan. Bake at 350° for 30 to 35 minutes. Spread warm brownies with Coffee Glaze; cool. Cut into bars. Makes 16.

Coffee Glaze: Stir together 2 teaspoons instant coffee crystals and 2 teaspoons milk till crystals dissolve. Stir in ¾ cup sifted powdered sugar. Stir in enough milk (about 1 teaspoon) till of spreading consistency.

Spicy Applesauce Brownies

    ½ cup shortening
    1¼ cups granulated sugar
    2 eggs
    ½ cup applesauce
    2 1-ounce squares unsweetened
        chocolate, melted and cooled
    1 teaspoon vanilla
    1 cup all-purpose flour
    1 teaspoon baking powder
    ½ teaspoon salt
    ½ teaspoon ground cinnamon
    ½ cup chopped walnuts
        • • •
    ¾ cup sifted powdered sugar
    ⅛ teaspoon ground cinnamon
        Milk

Cream shortening and granulated sugar; beat in eggs. Blend in applesauce, chocolate, and vanilla. Stir together flour, baking powder, salt, and ½ teaspoon cinnamon; stir into creamed mixture. Mix in chopped walnuts.

Spread in greased 13x9x2-inch baking pan. Bake at 350° for 25 minutes. Combine powdered sugar, ⅛ teaspoon cinnamon, and enough milk (about 4 teaspoons) till of drizzling consistency. Drizzle over slightly warm brownies. Cool; cut into bars. Makes 36.

Cookie Jar Classics

Keeping the cookie jar filled always has been a challenge to homemakers. And it will continue to be when you have any one of the taste-tempting cookies in this section on hand. The vast selection included here allows you to choose a recipe that not only suits the occasion, no matter what it is, but also adapts to time schedules as well.

Most cookies are made from similar basic ingredients in varying amounts and differ mainly in the way they are shaped. Some are dropped from a spoon. Other doughs are prepared in advance, refrigerated, then sliced and baked as needed. Versatile roll-and-bake cookies make use of cookie cutters for their shape, sometimes with added fillings. Still others are shaped by hand or formed with a cookie press. Whatever the shaping method specified, the cookies are guaranteed delicious. They'll inspire you to keep the cookie jar full.

Fill cookie containers with (clockwise, starting at top left): *Orange-Chocolate Chippers, Chocolate Pretzels, Grandmother's Jelly Cookies,* or *Coconut-Almond Dreams* and watch the cookies disappear. (See Index for page numbers.)

Easy Drop Cookies

Orange-Chocolate Chippers

A fun variation as shown on pages 34 and 35—

   1 cup shortening
   2 3-ounce packages cream cheese,
      softened
   ½ cup granulated sugar
   ½ cup packed brown sugar
   2 eggs
   2 teaspoons grated orange peel
   1 teaspoon vanilla
   2 cups all-purpose flour
   2 teaspoons baking powder
   1 teaspoon salt
   1 6-ounce package semisweet chocolate
      pieces (1 cup)
   ½ cup finely chopped nuts (optional)

Cream together shortening, cheese, and sugars. Add eggs, peel, and vanilla; beat well. Stir together flour, baking powder, and salt; add to creamed mixture. Mix well. Stir in chocolate. Drop from teaspoon 2 inches apart on ungreased cookie sheet. If desired, sprinkle lightly with nuts *or* granulated sugar. Bake at 350° about 10 minutes. Makes about 6 dozen.

Lemon-Pineapple Drops

   ½ cup shortening
   2 eggs
   1 3-ounce package lemon-flavored
      gelatin
   1 package pound cake mix
   1 8¼-ounce can crushed pineapple,
      well drained

In mixing bowl combine shortening and eggs; blend in gelatin. Add *half* of the cake mix; beat at medium speed of electric mixer till fluffy. Add remaining mix; blend on low speed, scraping sides of bowl constantly. Stir in fruit. Drop rounded teaspoonfuls 2 inches apart on ungreased cookie sheet. Bake at 375° for 10 to 12 minutes. Cool 1 to 2 minutes; remove from cookie sheet. Makes about 4 dozen.

Applesauce Cookies

   1 package 2-layer-size spice cake mix
   1 cup raisins
   ½ cup cooking oil
   ½ cup applesauce
   1 egg

In large mixing bowl combine spice cake mix, raisins, cooking oil, applesauce, and egg; beat at medium speed of electric mixer for 1 minute. Drop from teaspoon 2 inches apart on ungreased cookie sheet. Bake cookies at 350° for 12 to 15 minutes. Makes 6 dozen.

Sunflower-Chip Cookies

Whole wheat flour and sunflower seeds add character to this chocolate chip cookie version—

   ¼ cup butter *or* margarine, softened
   ¾ cup packed brown sugar
   2 eggs
   2 tablespoons rum *or* water
   ½ teaspoon vanilla
   1½ cups whole wheat flour
   ¼ cup nonfat dry milk powder
   ½ teaspoon baking soda
   ½ teaspoon salt
         • • •
   1 6-ounce package semisweet chocolate
      pieces (1 cup)
   ½ cup shelled sunflower seeds
   ¼ cup chopped peanuts

In mixer bowl cream together butter or margarine and brown sugar. Blend in eggs, rum, and vanilla; beat at medium speed of electric mixer for 2 minutes. (Mixture will be thin.) Thoroughly stir together whole wheat flour, dry milk powder, baking soda, and salt. Add to creamed mixture, blending well.

Stir in semisweet chocolate pieces, sunflower seeds, and chopped peanuts. Drop from teaspoon 2 inches apart on greased cookie sheet. Bake at 375° till done, 8 to 10 minutes. Makes about 3 dozen cookies.

Applesauce Cookies are quick-as-a-wink to prepare. Made with only five ingredients, one of which is a spice cake mix, they are assembled in one mixing step. Serve these raisin-rich nuggets to hungry children with glasses of ice cold milk for a nourishing after-school snack.

Chocolate Chippers

- ½ cup shortening
- ½ cup granulated sugar
- ¼ cup packed brown sugar
- 1 egg
- 1 teaspoon vanilla
- 1 cup all-purpose flour
- ¾ teaspoon salt
- ½ teaspoon baking soda
- 1 6-ounce package semisweet chocolate pieces (1 cup)
- ½ cup broken nuts

Cream together shortening, sugars, egg, and vanilla till light and fluffy. Thoroughly stir together flour, salt, and baking soda; stir into creamed mixture. Blend well. Stir in chocolate and nuts. Drop from teaspoon 2 inches apart on greased cookie sheet. Bake at 375° for 10 to 12 minutes. Immediately remove from cookie sheet to cool. Makes 3 dozen.

Sweet Chocolate Chip Cookies

- ½ cup butter *or* margarine, softened
- ⅓ cup granulated sugar
- ⅓ cup packed brown sugar
- 1 egg
- 1 tablespoon water
- ½ teaspoon vanilla
- 1¼ cups all-purpose flour
- ½ teaspoon baking soda
- ¼ teaspoon salt
- 2 4-ounce packages sweet cooking chocolate, coarsely chipped
- ½ cup chopped walnuts

Thoroughly cream together butter and sugars. Add egg, water, and vanilla; beat well. Stir together flour, soda, and salt; blend into creamed mixture. By hand, stir in chocolate and nuts. Drop from teaspoon 2 inches apart on greased cookie sheet. Bake at 350° about 15 minutes. Cool. Makes 3½ dozen.

Double Chocolate Drops

2¼ cups Basic Cookie Mix (see recipe,
      page 14)
1 egg
¼ cup milk
2 1-ounce squares unsweetened
      chocolate, melted and cooled
½ cup semisweet chocolate pieces
½ cup chopped nuts

Combine first 3 ingredients; beat well. Blend in cooled chocolate. Stir in chocolate pieces and nuts. Drop from teaspoon 2 inches apart on greased cookie sheet. Bake at 375° for 10 to 12 minutes. Remove cookies to rack; cool. If desired, frost with canned ready-to-spread vanilla *or* chocolate frosting. Makes 30.

Oatmeal-Raisin Cookies

2½ cups Basic Cookie Mix (see recipe,
      page 14)
2 beaten eggs
½ cup milk
¼ cup packed brown sugar
½ teaspoon ground cinnamon
½ teaspoon ground nutmeg
1 cup quick-cooking rolled oats
1 cup raisins

Combine first 6 ingredients; beat well. Stir in oats and raisins. Drop from teaspoon 2 inches apart on greased cookie sheet. Bake at 375° for 8 to 10 minutes. Makes 3 dozen.

Brown-Eyed Susan Cookies

1½ cups packaged biscuit mix
2 3⅝- or 3¾-ounce packages *instant*
      vanilla pudding mix
2 eggs
¼ cup butter *or* margarine, melted
   Milk chocolate candy stars

Combine biscuit and pudding mixes. Add eggs and butter; mix well. Drop from teaspoon on ungreased cookie sheet. Bake at 350° for 10 to 12 minutes. Immediately press a candy star on top of each cookie. Makes 3½ dozen.

Orange-Coconut Drops

2½ cups Basic Cookie Mix (see recipe,
      page 14)
¼ cup orange marmalade
1 egg
3 tablespoons orange juice
1 cup flaked coconut

In mixing bowl combine first 4 ingredients; beat well. Stir in flaked coconut. Drop from teaspoon 2 inches apart on greased cookie sheet. Bake at 375° for 8 to 10 minutes. If desired, frost cooled cookies with canned ready-to-spread orange frosting. Makes 30.

Crispy Chocolate Drops

Melt one 6-ounce package semisweet chocolate pieces over low heat; stir constantly. Remove from heat; stir in 2 cups crisp rice cereal and ½ cup chopped nuts. Drop from teaspoon on ungreased cookie sheet. Chill till firm. Store in refrigerator. Makes about 40.

Butterscotch Drops

1 6-ounce package butterscotch pieces
½ cup creamy peanut butter
3 cups presweetened cereal flakes

In top of double boiler over *hot, not boiling, water* heat first 2 ingredients; stir smooth. Remove from heat; stir in cereal till well coated. Drop from teaspoon on waxed paper-lined cookie sheet. Chill until firm. Makes 3 dozen.

Lacy Oatmeal Crisps

In saucepan combine 1 cup packed brown sugar, ½ cup shortening, and ¼ cup butter *or* margarine. Cook and stir over low heat till melted; remove from heat. Stir in 2 cups quick-cooking rolled oats, ½ teaspoon baking soda, and ¼ teaspoon salt. Add 1 well-beaten egg; mix well. Drop from teaspoon 3 inches apart on ungreased cookie sheet; stir remaining batter often. Bake at 375° for 6 to 7 minutes. Cool 2 minutes; gently remove to rack. Makes 48.

Spicy Cereal Crisps

Chewy while warm, but crispy when cooled—

½ cup shortening
½ cup packed brown sugar
1 teaspoon grated orange peel
½ cup honey
1 egg
1 cup all-purpose flour
1 teaspoon baking powder
1 teaspoon salt
½ teaspoon baking soda
½ teaspoon ground cinnamon
½ teaspoon ground nutmeg
½ teaspoon ground allspice
⅛ teaspoon ground cloves
1 cup quick-cooking rolled oats
½ cup cornflakes
½ cup chopped walnuts

Cream together shortening, sugar, and peel; beat in honey and egg. Stir together flour and next 7 ingredients. Add to creamed mixture with oats, cornflakes, and nuts; mix well. Drop from teaspoon on greased cookie sheet. Bake at 375° for 12 to 14 minutes. Makes 36.

Peanut-Oatmeal Drops

Chopped peanuts add flavor and crunch—

¾ cup shortening
½ cup peanut butter
¾ cup packed brown sugar
½ cup granulated sugar
3 eggs
¼ cup milk
1 teaspoon vanilla
1½ cups all-purpose flour
1 teaspoon baking soda
½ teaspoon salt
1 cup quick-cooking rolled oats
1 cup chopped peanuts

Cream together shortening, peanut butter, and sugars till light and fluffy; add eggs one at a time, beating well after each. Blend in milk and vanilla. Thoroughly stir together flour, soda, and salt; stir into creamed mixture. Stir in oats and peanuts. Drop from teaspoon 2 inches apart on greased cookie sheet. Bake at 350° for 10 to 12 minutes. Makes 6 dozen.

Peach Drops

½ cup butter *or* margarine, softened
1 3-ounce package cream cheese, softened
¼ cup packed brown sugar
½ cup peach preserves
1¼ cups all-purpose flour
1½ teaspoons baking powder
1 teaspoon ground cinnamon
¼ teaspoon salt
½ cup chopped walnuts

• • •

1 cup sifted powdered sugar
¼ cup peach preserves
1 tablespoon butter *or* margarine, softened

Cream together ½ cup butter, cream cheese, and brown sugar till light and fluffy. Beat in ½ cup preserves. Stir together flour, baking powder, cinnamon, and salt; stir into creamed mixture. Blend in nuts. Drop level tablespoonfuls on greased cookie sheet. Bake at 350° till lightly browned, about 12 minutes. Cool.

Blend together powdered sugar, ¼ cup peach preserves, and 1 tablespoon butter; beat well. Spread frosting atop cooled cookies. Makes 2 to 2½ dozen.

Pineapple-Coconut Drops

½ cup butter *or* margarine, softened
½ cup granulated sugar
½ cup packed brown sugar
1 8¼-ounce can crushed pineapple, well drained
1 egg
1 teaspoon vanilla
2 cups all-purpose flour
1 teaspoon baking powder
¼ teaspoon baking soda
¼ teaspoon salt
½ cup shredded coconut

Cream butter and sugars till fluffy; beat in pineapple, egg, and vanilla. Stir together flour, baking powder, soda, and salt; stir into creamed mixture. Blend in coconut. Drop from teaspoon on greased cookie sheet. Bake at 375° about 8 minutes. Makes about 42.

Orange Drop Cookies

Topped with pecan halves as shown on page 89 —

    ¾ cup shortening
    ¼ cup butter *or* margarine, softened
    1½ cups packed brown sugar
    2 eggs
    1 cup buttermilk
    2 tablespoons grated orange peel
    ¼ cup orange juice
    1 teaspoon vanilla
    3½ cups all-purpose flour
    2 teaspoons baking powder
    1 teaspoon baking soda
    ¼ teaspoon salt
    1 cup chopped pecans
    Pecan halves

Cream first 3 ingredients; beat in eggs. Slowly beat in buttermilk, peel, juice, and vanilla. Stir together flour, baking powder, soda, and salt; blend into batter. Stir in chopped pecans. Drop from teaspoon on greased cookie sheet. Place pecan half on each cookie. Bake at 350° about 15 minutes. Makes 8 dozen.

Apricot-Bran Drops

    ¾ cup finely chopped dried apricots
    ½ cup orange juice
    ½ cup whole bran cereal
    ½ cup butter *or* margarine, softened
    ½ cup packed brown sugar
    ½ cup granulated sugar
    1 egg
    1 teaspoon vanilla
    1½ cups all-purpose flour
    1 teaspoon baking powder
    ¾ teaspoon ground cinnamon
    ⅓ cup chopped nuts

Pour boiling water over apricots; cool. Mix juice and cereal; let stand 5 minutes. Cream butter and sugars; beat in egg and vanilla. Stir cereal mixture into creamed mixture. Stir together flour, baking powder, cinnamon, and ½ teaspoon salt; stir into creamed mixture. Drain apricots well; fold with nuts into creamed mixture. Drop from teaspoon on greased cookie sheet. Bake at 375° till lightly browned, about 10 minutes. Makes 4½ dozen.

Wheat Germ-Date Cookies

    1 8-ounce package finely snipped
        pitted dates (1⅓ cups)
    ½ cup light molasses
    ½ cup honey
    ½ cup cooking oil
    2 eggs
    1 teaspoon vanilla
    1 teaspoon grated orange peel
    2 cups all-purpose flour
    ⅓ cup wheat germ
    1 teaspoon salt
    1 teaspoon ground cinnamon
    ½ teaspoon baking powder
    ½ teaspoon baking soda
    ⅓ cup shelled sunflower seeds

In saucepan combine dates, molasses, honey, and 2 tablespoons water; simmer 2 minutes. Remove from heat. Stir in oil; cool. Beat in eggs, vanilla, and peel. Stir together flour and next 5 ingredients; stir into date mixture. Blend in sunflower seeds. Drop from teaspoon 2 inches apart on greased cookie sheet. Bake at 375° for 7 to 8 minutes. Makes 78.

Pumpkin Cookies

    2 cups shortening
    2 cups sugar
    1 16-ounce can pumpkin
    2 eggs
    2 teaspoons vanilla
    4 cups all-purpose flour
    2 teaspoons baking powder
    2 teaspoons ground cinnamon
    1 teaspoon baking soda
    1 teaspoon ground nutmeg
    ½ teaspoon ground allspice
    2 cups raisins
    1 cup chopped nuts

Cream shortening and sugar. Add pumpkin, eggs, and vanilla; beat well. Stir together flour, next 5 ingredients, and 1 teaspoon salt. Add to batter; mix well. Stir in raisins and nuts. Drop rounded teaspoonfuls 2 inches apart on greased cookie sheet. Bake at 350° for 12 to 15 minutes. Cool on rack. If desired, frost with vanilla frosting. Makes 7 dozen.

Carrot Cookies

    2 cups diced, peeled carrots
    ¾ cup butter *or* margarine, softened
    1 cup sugar
    1 egg
    1 teaspoon vanilla
    2 cups all-purpose flour
    2 teaspoons baking powder
    ½ teaspoon salt
       Pineapple Frosting (see recipe,
          page 18)

Cook carrots in small amount of boiling salted water till tender; drain and mash. (Should measure about 1 cup.) Cool. Cream butter and sugar. Add egg and vanilla; beat till fluffy. Stir in mashed carrots. Stir together flour, baking powder, and salt; blend into batter. Drop from teaspoon on ungreased cookie sheet. Bake at 375° about 12 minutes. Cool; spread with Pineapple Frosting. Makes about 5 dozen.

Two-Tone Cookies

    6 tablespoons butter *or* margarine,
          softened
    ½ cup packed brown sugar
    ¼ cup granulated sugar
    ½ teaspoon vanilla
    1 egg
    ½ cup dairy sour cream
    1¼ cups all-purpose flour
    ½ teaspoon salt
    ¼ teaspoon baking soda
    ¼ cup chopped walnuts
    1 1-ounce square unsweetened
          chocolate, melted and cooled

Cream first 4 ingredients. Add egg; beat till fluffy. Stir in sour cream. Stir together flour, salt, and soda. Gradually mix into creamed mixture; stir in nuts. Divide dough in half; stir chocolate into one portion. Drop rounded teaspoonfuls of chocolate dough 2 inches apart on ungreased cookie sheet. Drop rounded teaspoonfuls of plain dough next to chocolate mounds. (They will bake together as one.) If desired, press a walnut half atop each cookie. Bake at 375° for 12 to 15 minutes. Cool on rack. Makes 1½ to 2 dozen.

Date-Filled Drop Cookies

A quick and easy way to make a filled cookie—

    1 8-ounce package finely snipped
          pitted dates (1⅓ cups)
    ½ cup granulated sugar
    ½ cup water
    2 teaspoons lemon juice
    ½ cup chopped nuts
          • • •
    1 cup shortening
    1½ cups packed brown sugar
    3 eggs
    1 teaspoon vanilla
    3½ cups all-purpose flour
    1 teaspoon baking soda
    ½ teaspoon salt
    ¼ teaspoon ground cinnamon
    ¼ cup milk

In saucepan combine finely snipped dates, granulated sugar, and water; cook till mixture is thick, stirring frequently. Remove from heat; stir in lemon juice and nuts. Cool. Cream together shortening and brown sugar till fluffy; add eggs, one at a time, beating well after each. Beat in vanilla. Thoroughly stir together flour, baking soda, salt, and cinnamon. Add dry ingredients alternately with milk to creamed mixture; mix well.

Drop scant teaspoonfuls of dough 2 inches apart on greased cookie sheet. Top each cookie with about ½ *teaspoon* date mixture; cover with another scant teaspoonful of dough. Bake at 375° for 10 to 12 minutes. Makes 48.

TEST KITCHEN TIP

Drop small mounds of each type of batter side-by-side on cookie sheet to make dual-flavored *Two-Tone Cookies.* During baking, the batters bake together as one.

TEST KITCHEN TIP

Candy-centered *Meringue Kisses* hide a surprise inside each cookie. Use a knife or narrow spatula to swirl meringue over candy, making certain it is well covered.

Meringue Kisses

    3 egg whites
    1 teaspoon vanilla
  ¼ teaspoon cream of tartar
  ¼ teaspoon peppermint extract
      (optional)
      Dash salt
    1 cup granulated sugar
  36 milk chocolate candies
      Green sugar crystals

In small mixing bowl beat whites with vanilla, cream of tartar, extract, and salt till soft peaks form. Very slowly add 1 cup granulated sugar; beat till very stiff but not dry. Drop from tablespoon 1½ inches apart on ungreased cookie sheet. Press a candy into each cookie. With knife or narrow spatula, bring meringue up and over candy; swirl top. Sprinkle with green sugar. Bake at 275° for 30 minutes. Immediately remove cookies to rack. Makes 36.

Pecan Drops

Cream together 1 cup softened butter and 1¼ cups sifted powdered sugar till fluffy. Blend in 1 teaspoon vanilla. Stir together 2⅓ cups all-purpose flour and ½ teaspoon salt; stir into creamed mixture alternately with ⅓ cup milk. Stir in 1 cup coarsely chopped pecans. Drop from teaspoon 2 inches apart on ungreased cookie sheet. Bake at 325° for 15 to 20 minutes. Makes about 4 dozen.

Coconut Crunch Cookies

    1 cup shortening
    1 cup packed brown sugar
  ½ cup granulated sugar
    2 eggs
    2 tablespoons milk
    1 teaspoon vanilla
    2 cups all-purpose flour
    1 teaspoon baking soda
    1 teaspoon salt
  ½ cup chopped walnuts
    3 1⅝-ounce chocolate-coated coconut
      candy bars, chilled and coarsely
      chopped (about 1 cup)

Cream shortening and sugars. Add eggs, milk, and vanilla; beat till fluffy. Stir together flour, soda, and salt; blend into creamed mixture. Stir in nuts; gently fold in candy. Drop from tablespoon 2 inches apart on ungreased cookie sheet.* Bake at 375° for 10 to 12 minutes. Cool cookies on rack. Makes 4 dozen.

  *Or, chill dough 30 minutes; form into 1-inch balls. Place on ungreased cookie sheet; bake at 375° for 12 to 14 minutes. Cool on rack.

Apple-Raisin Cookies

  ½ cup butter *or* margarine, softened
    1 cup packed brown sugar
    2 eggs
  ¼ cup milk
    2 cups all-purpose flour
    1 teaspoon baking powder
    1 teaspoon ground cinnamon
  ½ teaspoon salt
  ½ teaspoon ground nutmeg
  ¼ teaspoon ground cloves
    2 medium apples, peeled, cored, and
      chopped (1½ cups)
    1 cup raisins
  ½ cup chopped walnuts

Cream butter and sugar. Add eggs and milk; beat well. Stir together flour and next 5 ingredients; stir into creamed mixture. Stir in apples, raisins, and nuts. Drop from tablespoon on well-greased cookie sheet. Bake at 350° for 12 to 14 minutes. Immediately remove cookies to rack. Makes 4½ dozen.

Crispy Almond-Coconut Drops

See footnote on page 25 for toasting nuts—

In mixing bowl beat 2 eggs till thick and lemon-colored. Gradually blend in 1 cup sugar; beat till very thick. Blend in ½ teaspoon vanilla and ¼ teaspoon almond extract. Stir together ½ cup all-purpose flour and ⅛ teaspoon salt; blend into egg mixture. Stir in 2 cups finely chopped blanched almonds, toasted (about 8 ounces), and 1 cup shredded coconut. Let stand 15 minutes. Drop from teaspoon on ungreased foil-lined cookie sheet. Bake at 325° for 15 to 18 minutes. Makes 5 dozen.

Coconut Macaroons

> 2 egg whites
> ½ teaspoon vanilla
>   Dash salt
> ⅔ cup sugar
> 1 3½-ounce can flaked coconut
>   (1⅓ cups)

Beat egg whites with vanilla and salt till soft peaks form. Gradually add sugar, beating till stiff but not dry. Fold in coconut. Drop rounded teaspoonfuls on greased cookie sheet. Bake at 325° about 20 minutes. Immediately remove cookies to rack. Makes 18.

Filbert Macaroons

Beat powdered sugar into egg whites at high speed of electric mixer till batter resembles divinity—

> 1 3½-ounce package whole unblanched
>   filberts (¾ cup)
> 2 egg whites
> 1 teaspoon lemon juice
> 1 cup sifted powdered sugar
> ¼ teaspoon ground cinnamon

Grind filberts, using coarse blade of food grinder; set aside. In small mixer bowl beat egg whites with lemon juice till stiff peaks form. Gradually beat in sugar and cinnamon. Fold in nuts. Drop rounded teaspoonfuls on greased cookie sheet. If desired, top each with a whole filbert. Bake at 350° for 10 to 15 minutes. Immediately remove to rack. Makes 24.

Frosted Cashew Drops

> ½ cup butter *or* margarine, softened
> 1 cup packed brown sugar
> 1 egg
> ½ teaspoon vanilla
> 2 cups all-purpose flour
> ¾ teaspoon baking soda
> ¾ teaspoon baking powder
> ½ teaspoon ground cinnamon
> ¼ teaspoon salt
> ¼ teaspoon ground nutmeg
> ⅓ cup dairy sour cream
> 1 cup chopped cashew nuts
>   • • •
> 3 tablespoons butter *or* margarine
> 2 cups sifted powdered sugar
> 2 tablespoons milk
> 1 teaspoon vanilla

In mixing bowl cream together ½ cup butter and brown sugar. Add egg and ½ teaspoon vanilla; beat well. Thoroughly stir together flour, baking soda, baking powder, cinnamon, salt, and nutmeg. Add to creamed mixture alternately with sour cream. Stir in cashews. Drop from teaspoon 2 inches apart on greased cookie sheet. Bake at 400° till lightly browned, 8 to 10 minutes. Immediately remove cookies from cookie sheet to cooling rack.

In small saucepan heat and stir 3 tablespoons butter or margarine till browned. Slowly beat in powdered sugar, milk, and 1 teaspoon vanilla. Spread frosting over tops of cooled cookies. Makes 4 dozen.

TEST KITCHEN TIP

When dropping batter on cookie sheet, allow ample room for cookies to spread during baking. Generally, thin batters will spread more than thick batters.

Refrigerator Cookies

44

Chocolate-Coconut Slices

Coconut Filling
6 tablespoons butter, softened
1 cup sifted powdered sugar
1 egg
2 1-ounce squares unsweetened
chocolate, melted and cooled
1 teaspoon vanilla
1½ cups all-purpose flour
½ teaspoon baking soda

Prepare Coconut Filling; chill. Cream butter and sugar; blend in egg, chocolate, and vanilla. Stir together flour, soda, and ½ teaspoon salt; stir into creamed mixture. Chill 30 minutes. Between two pieces of waxed paper, roll dough to 14x4-inch rectangle. Remove top paper. Shape filling into a log 14 inches long. Place log atop rectangle; roll dough around filling. Seal edges. Wrap in waxed paper or clear plastic wrap. Chill well. Cut into ¼-inch slices. Place on greased cookie sheet. Bake at 375° for 8 to 10 minutes. Cool 1 minute; gently remove to rack. Makes about 4½ dozen.

Coconut Filling: In small mixing bowl blend together one 3-ounce package softened cream cheese, ⅓ cup granulated sugar, and 1 teaspoon vanilla till smooth. Stir in 1 cup cookie coconut *or* finely chopped flaked coconut and ½ cup finely chopped nuts.

Lemon-Chip Cookies

Cream 1 cup softened butter with 1 cup sugar. Beat in 1 egg, 1½ teaspoons shredded lemon peel, 1 tablespoon lemon juice, and 1 tablespoon water. Stir together 2¾ cups all-purpose flour, ¼ teaspoon baking soda, and ¼ teaspoon salt; stir into creamed mixture. Stir in one 1-ounce square semisweet chocolate, grated (⅓ cup). Shape into two 9-inch rolls. Wrap in waxed paper or clear plastic wrap. Chill thoroughly. Cut into ¼-inch slices. Place on ungreased cookie sheet. Bake at 375° for 10 to 12 minutes. Makes about 6 dozen.

Golden Raisin Whirls

⅓ cup sugar
2 tablespoons cornstarch
⅓ cup water
1 cup light raisins, ground
1 teaspoon grated lemon peel
• • •
1 3-ounce package cream cheese,
softened
¼ cup butter *or* margarine, softened
⅔ cup sugar
1 egg
1 tablespoon lemon juice
• • •
1¾ cups all-purpose flour
½ teaspoon salt
¼ teaspoon baking soda

In saucepan combine ⅓ cup sugar and cornstarch; stir in water. Add ground raisins. Cook over medium heat, stirring constantly, till mixture thickens and bubbles. Remove filling from heat; stir in lemon peel. Cool.

In mixing bowl cream together cream cheese, butter or margarine, and ⅔ cup sugar till light and fluffy. Blend in egg and lemon juice. Thoroughly stir together flour, salt, and baking soda; stir into creamed mixture.

Divide dough in half. On waxed paper, roll *half* of the dough to 11x7-inch rectangle; spread dough with *half* of the raisin filling. Roll rectangle jelly-roll fashion beginning at long side; pinch edges to seal. Wrap in waxed paper or clear plastic wrap. Repeat with remaining dough and filling. Chill thoroughly.

Cut into ¼-inch slices. Place on greased cookie sheet. Bake at 375° till lightly browned, 10 to 12 minutes. Makes about 7 dozen.

Refrigerator cookies let you bake cookies as ▶ you need them. This assortment includes (front) *Chocolate-Coconut Slices* and *Golden Raisin Whirls*, (left) *Lemon-Chip Cookies*, and (right) *Cherry-Pecan Gems* (see recipe, page 46).

TEST KITCHEN TIP

To coat rolls of refrigerator cookie dough with nuts, spread finely chopped nuts on waxed paper and use a gentle rolling motion to add a uniform coating of nuts.

Sugar-Pecan Crisps

¾ cup butter *or* margarine, softened
⅔ cup sugar
1 egg
1 teaspoon vanilla
¼ teaspoon salt
1¾ cups all-purpose flour
• • •
½ cup finely chopped pecans

Cream together butter and sugar till light and fluffy. Beat in egg, vanilla, and salt. Gradually stir in flour. Cover and chill 30 minutes for easier handling. Shape dough into a 12-inch log; roll in chopped pecans to coat outside of log. Wrap in waxed paper or clear plastic wrap. Chill thoroughly. Cut into ¼-inch slices. Place on ungreased cookie sheet; bake at 350° till lightly browned, 10 to 12 minutes. Makes 4 dozen cookies.

Cinnamon-Nut Slices

1 roll refrigerated sugar cookie dough
½ cup chopped pecans
¾ teaspoon ground cinnamon

Slice refrigerated cookie dough into ¼-inch slices. Combine pecans and cinnamon; dip one side of cookies in pecan mixture. Place nut side up on ungreased cookie sheet. Bake at 375° till cookies are lightly browned, 8 to 10 minutes. Makes 3½ dozen.

Cherry-Pecan Gems

These cherry-topped cookies are shown on page 45—

1 cup butter *or* margarine, softened
1 cup sugar
1 egg
2 tablespoons red maraschino cherry syrup
¼ teaspoon almond extract
Few drops red food coloring
2½ cups all-purpose flour
1 teaspoon baking soda
½ teaspoon cream of tartar
1 cup finely chopped pecans
Red maraschino cherries, halved

Cream butter and sugar; blend in egg, syrup, extract, and food coloring. Stir together flour, soda, cream of tartar, and ¼ teaspoon salt; stir into creamed mixture. Stir in nuts. Shape dough into two 9-inch rolls. Wrap in waxed paper or clear plastic wrap. Chill well.

Cut into ¼-inch slices; place on ungreased cookie sheet. Lightly press a well-drained red maraschino cherry half in center of each cookie. (Omit cherries when cookies are stored.) Bake at 375° for 10 to 12 minutes. Cool slightly; remove to rack. Makes 6 dozen.

Vanilla Sugar Slices

½ cup butter *or* margarine, softened
¼ cup shortening
1¼ cups sifted powdered sugar
1 egg
1 teaspoon vanilla
2 cups all-purpose flour
1 teaspoon baking powder
½ teaspoon salt
¼ teaspoon baking soda

Cream butter, shortening, and sugar; blend in egg and vanilla. Stir together flour, baking powder, salt, and soda; stir into creamed mixture.. Shape into two 6½-inch rolls. Wrap in waxed paper or clear plastic wrap. Chill well. Cut into ¼-inch slices; place on ungreased cookie sheet. If desired, press a pecan half in center of each cookie *or* sprinkle with granulated sugar. Bake at 375° for 8 to 10 minutes. Makes about 4 dozen.

Oatmeal Refrigerator Cookies

For square cookies, pack dough into any empty foil, waxed paper, or plastic wrap box lined with foil—

>   1 cup shortening
>   1 cup granulated sugar
>   1 cup packed brown sugar
>   2 eggs
>   1 teaspoon vanilla
> 1½ cups all-purpose flour
>   1 teaspoon salt
>   1 teaspoon baking soda
>   1 teaspoon ground cinnamon
> 1½ cups quick-cooking rolled oats
>   ½ cup finely chopped walnuts

Cream together shortening, granulated sugar, and brown sugar till light and fluffy. Add eggs, one at a time, beating well after each; add vanilla. Thoroughly stir together flour, salt, baking soda, and cinnamon; stir into creamed mixture. Stir in oats and walnuts. Shape dough into two 8-inch rolls. Wrap in waxed paper or clear plastic wrap. Chill thoroughly. Cut into ¼-inch slices. Place on greased cookie sheet. Bake at 350° for 8 to 10 minutes. Makes about 5 dozen cookies.

Orange Refrigerator Cookies

>   1 cup butter *or* margarine, softened
>   ½ cup granulated sugar
>   ½ cup packed brown sugar
>   1 egg
>   1 tablespoon grated orange peel
>   ¼ cup orange juice
>   1 teaspoon vanilla
>   3 cups all-purpose flour
>   ½ teaspoon salt
>   ¼ teaspoon baking soda
>   ½ cup finely chopped walnuts

Cream together butter, granulated sugar, and brown sugar. Add egg, peel, juice, and vanilla; beat well. Stir together flour, salt, and soda; add to creamed mixture. Mix well. Stir in walnuts. Shape into two 6½-inch rolls. Wrap in waxed paper or clear plastic wrap. Chill thoroughly. Cut into ⅛-inch slices. Place on ungreased cookie sheet. Bake at 375° for 12 to 15 minutes. Makes 8 dozen.

Gumdrop Cookies

>   1 cup butter *or* margarine, softened
>   ½ cup granulated sugar
>   ½ cup packed brown sugar
>   2 tablespoons milk
>   1 teaspoon vanilla
> • • •
> 2½ cups all-purpose flour
>   1 teaspoon baking powder
>   ¾ cup finely chopped gumdrops

Cream together butter and sugars; beat in milk and vanilla. Stir together flour and baking powder; blend into creamed mixture. Stir in gumdrops. Shape dough into two 14-inch rolls. Wrap in waxed paper or clear plastic wrap. Chill thoroughly. Cut into ¼-inch slices. Place on ungreased cookie sheet. Bake at 375° about 10 minutes. Makes about 9 dozen.

Ginger-Molasses Crisps

Cream 1 cup shortening and ¾ cup packed brown sugar. Blend in ⅓ cup dark molasses, 1 egg, and 1 teaspoon vanilla. Stir together 2¾ cups all-purpose flour, 1 teaspoon salt, 1 teaspoon baking powder, 1 teaspoon ground ginger, and ½ teaspoon baking soda; stir into creamed mixture. Chill at least 30 minutes.

Shape soft dough into two 9½-inch rolls. Wrap in waxed paper or clear plastic wrap. Chill thoroughly. Cut into ¼-inch slices. Place on ungreased cookie sheet. Bake at 350° for 8 to 10 minutes. Makes about 6 dozen.

Health Cookies

Toast sesame seed at 350° for 10 minutes; stir—

Blend ½ cup safflower *or* peanut oil with ¾ cup packed brown sugar; beat in 1 egg and 1 teaspoon vanilla. Stir together 1¾ cups all-purpose flour, ½ teaspoon salt, and ¼ teaspoon baking soda; stir into sugar mixture. Stir in ¼ cup sesame seed, toasted, and ¼ cup wheat germ. Shape dough into two 9-inch rolls. Wrap in waxed paper or clear plastic wrap. Chill thoroughly. Cut into ¼-inch slices. Place cookies on ungreased cookie sheet. Bake at 350° about 10 minutes. Makes 6 dozen.

Coconut-Almond Dreams

Egg yolk glaze bakes to a golden brown atop these cookies as pictured on pages 34 and 35—

    1 cup butter *or* margarine, softened
    1 cup sugar
    1 egg
    ½ teaspoon almond extract
    1 3½-ounce can flaked coconut
        (1⅓ cups)
    2¼ cups all-purpose flour
    ½ teaspoon baking soda
    1 egg yolk
    1 tablespoon milk
    Almond *or* pecan halves, toasted

Cream butter and sugar; beat in egg and extract. Stir in *1 cup* of the coconut. Stir flour with soda and ½ teaspoon salt; add to creamed mixture. Mix well. Knead in bowl till dough clings together. Shape into three 8-inch logs; roll in remaining coconut. Wrap in waxed paper or clear plastic wrap. Chill well. With sharp knife, cut *each* roll into 24 slices. Place 2 inches apart on ungreased cookie sheet. Beat yolk with milk; brush over cookies. Lightly press a nut atop each cookie. *(See footnote on page 25 for toasting nuts.)* Bake at 325° for 17 to 20 minutes. Makes 6 dozen cookies.

Spicy Nut Slices

    1 cup butter *or* margarine, softened
    1 cup packed brown sugar
    ½ cup granulated sugar
    2 eggs
    1 teaspoon vanilla
    2¾ cups all-purpose flour
    1 teaspoon ground cinnamon
    ½ teaspoon baking soda
    ¼ teaspoon ground allspice
    1 cup finely chopped almonds

Cream butter and sugars. Add eggs; beat well. Blend in vanilla. Stir flour with next 3 ingredients and ½ teaspoon salt; stir into creamed mixture. Add nuts. Shape into two 9-inch rolls. Wrap in waxed paper or clear plastic wrap. Chill well. Cut into ¼-inch slices; place on ungreased cookie sheet. Bake at 375° about 8 minutes. Cool 1 minute; remove. Makes 72.

Date Pinwheels

    Date-Nut Filling
    ½ cup shortening
    1 cup packed brown sugar
    2 eggs
    ½ teaspoon vanilla
    2⅓ cups all-purpose flour
    ½ teaspoon baking powder
    ¼ teaspoon baking soda
    ¼ teaspoon salt
    ¼ teaspoon ground cinnamon

Prepare Date-Nut Filling; chill. Cream shortening and sugar; beat in eggs and vanilla. Combine flour and remaining ingredients; stir into creamed mixture. Chill dough 30 minutes.

On waxed paper, roll dough to 18x10-inch rectangle. Spread with filling. Roll rectangle jelly-roll fashion beginning at long side; pinch edges together to seal. Cut roll in half crosswise. Wrap each roll in waxed paper or clear plastic wrap. Chill thoroughly.

Carefully cut into ¼-inch slices. Place on greased cookie sheet. Bake at 350° till lightly browned, 8 to 10 minutes. Makes 6 dozen.

Date-Nut Filling: In small saucepan combine one 8-ounce package finely snipped pitted dates (1⅓ cups), ⅓ cup granulated sugar, and ⅓ cup water; bring to boil. Cook and stir over low heat till thickened, about 4 minutes. Remove from heat; stir in ½ cup finely chopped nuts and ½ teaspoon vanilla.

Saucepan Date Rounds

In saucepan melt 2 tablespoons butter *or* margarine; stir in 1 cup granulated sugar. Add 1 cup finely chopped pitted dates and 2 beaten eggs. Cook and stir over low heat till thick and bubbly, about 7 minutes. Stir in 3 cups crisp rice cereal, ½ cup finely chopped nuts, 2 tablespoons finely chopped candied orange peel, and 1 teaspoon vanilla; mix well. Cool to room temperature. On waxed paper sprinkled with powdered sugar, form mixture into two 7-inch rolls.* Wrap in waxed paper or clear plastic wrap. Chill thoroughly. Cut into ¼-inch slices. Makes about 4½ dozen.

*Or, shape mixture into small balls or logs. Roll in powdered sugar and chill thoroughly.

Fruit-Filled Rounds

Cream together ½ cup softened butter *or* margarine and ½ cup packed brown sugar; beat in 1 egg. Stir together 1½ cups all-purpose flour, ½ teaspoon salt, and ¼ teaspoon baking soda. Stir into creamed mixture. Shape dough into a 10-inch roll. Wrap in waxed paper or clear plastic wrap. Chill thoroughly.

In saucepan combine 1 cup diced unpeeled apple, ½ cup granulated sugar, ¼ cup raisins, ¼ cup chopped nuts, 2 tablespoons water, and ½ teaspoon ground cinnamon. Cook and stir over medium heat till mixture is thickened and apple is tender, about 10 minutes. Chill.

Cut chilled rolls into ⅛-inch slices. Place *half* of the slices on ungreased cookie sheets. Top each with ¼ *teaspoon* of the apple filling. Cover filling with remaining cookie slices; seal edges with a fork. Bake at 375° for 8 to 10 minutes. Makes about 3½ dozen.

Cocoa-Mint Sandwiches

A chocolate-cream cookie children will enjoy—

   ¾ **cup butter** *or* **margarine, softened**
   1 **cup sugar**
   1 **egg**
   ½ **teaspoon vanilla**
   2 **cups all-purpose flour**
   ¾ **cup unsweetened cocoa powder**
   1 **teaspoon baking powder**
   ½ **teaspoon baking soda**
   ¼ **cup milk**
      Mint Filling

Cream butter and sugar. Add egg and vanilla; beat well. Stir together flour, next 3 ingredients, and ½ teaspoon salt. Add to creamed mixture alternately with milk; mix well. Form into two 10-inch rolls. Wrap in waxed paper or clear plastic wrap. Chill well. Cut into ⅛-inch slices; place on ungreased cookie sheet. Bake at 325° for 10 minutes. Immediately remove to rack. Assemble cooled cookies, sandwich-style, with Mint Filling. Makes 6½ dozen.

Mint Filling: Combine 1½ cups sifted powdered sugar, 3 tablespoons softened butter *or* margarine, 1 tablespoon milk, 2 or 3 drops green food coloring, and 1 or 2 drops oil of peppermint. Blend till smooth and creamy.

Chocolate-Filled Pinwheels

Orange-flavored cookies with chocolate filling—

   ¾ **cup butter** *or* **margarine, softened**
   1 **cup sugar**
   1 **egg**
   1½ **teaspoons grated orange peel**
   1 **tablespoon orange juice**
   2 **cups all-purpose flour**
   1 **teaspoon baking powder**
   ½ **teaspoon salt**
   1 **6-ounce package semisweet chocolate**
      pieces (1 cup)
   2 **tablespoons butter** *or* **margarine**
   1 **cup finely chopped nuts**
   2 **tablespoons orange juice**

Cream first 2 ingredients; beat in egg, peel, and 1 tablespoon juice. Stir flour with baking powder and salt; stir into creamed mixture. Reserve ⅔ cup dough. Cover remaining dough; chill 1 hour. In saucepan melt chocolate and 2 tablespoons butter over low heat; stir occasionally. Remove from heat; stir in nuts, 2 tablespoons juice, and the reserved ⅔ cup of dough. Mix well.

On lightly floured surface, roll chilled dough to 16x12-inch rectangle; spread chocolate mixture over dough. Roll rectangle jelly-roll fashion beginning at long side; pinch edges to seal. Cut roll in half crosswise. Wrap each roll in waxed paper or clear plastic wrap. Chill well. Cut into ¼-inch slices. Place on ungreased cookie sheet. Bake at 350° for 10 to 12 minutes. Makes about 5 dozen.

TEST KITCHEN TIP

To assemble *Cocoa-Mint Sandwiches*, spread filling over bottoms of half of the baked chocolate slices. Place remaining cookies, bottom-side down, atop filling.

Roll-and-Bake Cookies

Cream Cheese Pastries

    1 cup butter *or* margarine, softened
    1 8-ounce package cream cheese,
        softened
    ½ cup sifted powdered sugar
    2 cups all-purpose flour
    ¼ teaspoon salt
    ⅓ cup tart red jelly *or* jam

Cream butter and cream cheese till fluffy; gradually blend in sugar. Stir together flour and salt; stir into creamed mixture. Cover; chill dough several hours or overnight.

Divide dough in thirds. On lightly floured surface, roll *each* portion to 12½x10-inch rectangle. With fluted pastry wheel, cut into 2½-inch squares. Place a dot of jelly in center of each square; bring up two diagonal corners to center, pinching together to seal.

Place on ungreased cookie sheet. Bake at 375° till firm but not brown, about 12 minutes. If desired, sift additional powdered sugar over slightly warm pastries. Makes 5 dozen.

Swedish Honey Cookies

    ½ cup butter *or* margarine, softened
    ⅔ cup packed brown sugar
    ⅓ cup honey
    1 egg
    2 cups all-purpose flour
    1 teaspoon ground coriander
    ½ teaspoon baking soda
    ½ teaspoon salt
    ¼ teaspoon ground cinnamon

Cream butter, sugar, and honey; beat in egg. Stir flour with remaining ingredients. Stir into creamed mixture, working to make a soft dough. Divide in half; wrap in waxed paper. Chill. On well-floured surface, roll *each* portion to ⅛-inch thickness. Cut into desired shapes with cookie cutter. Place on ungreased cookie sheet; bake at 375° till golden, 5 to 7 minutes. Makes about 4 dozen.

Butterhorn Spice Cookies

    1 package active dry yeast
    2 tablespoons warm water (110° F.)
    2 cups all-purpose flour
    ½ teaspoon ground nutmeg
    ½ teaspoon ground ginger
    ¼ teaspoon salt
    ½ cup butter *or* margarine, softened
    ½ cup dairy sour cream
    2 egg yolks
            • • •
    2 egg whites
    1 teaspoon ground cinnamon
    ½ cup granulated sugar
    ½ cup finely chopped walnuts
        Sifted powdered sugar

Soften yeast in warm water. In mixing bowl combine ¾ *cup* of the flour, nutmeg, ginger, and salt; cut in butter till mixture resembles fine crumbs. Combine sour cream, egg yolks, and softened yeast; add all at once to flour mixture. Beat at low speed with electric mixer for 1 minute, scraping sides of bowl constantly; beat 1 minute at high speed. Blend in remaining flour. Cover; chill 1 hour.

Beat egg whites with cinnamon till soft peaks form; gradually add granulated sugar, beating till stiff but not dry. Fold in nuts.

Divide chilled dough in half. On surface sprinkled with powdered sugar, roll *each* portion to an 11-inch circle; cut into 16 wedges. Spread *1 tablespoon* of the meringue on each wedge. Beginning at wide end of wedge, roll toward point. Place point down on greased cookie sheet. Bake at 400° till golden brown, 10 to 12 minutes. If desired, sift powdered sugar over slightly cooled cookies. Makes 32.

Master the rolling pin and you're on your way ▶ to offering a gala selection of sweets at your next coffee. This tempting trio includes jelly-dotted *Cream Cheese Pastries*, *Swedish Honey Cookies*, and *Butterhorn Spice Cookies*.

TEST KITCHEN TIP

To make *Sour Cream Pastries*, roll dough to a circle and top with filling ingredients. With fluted pastry wheel, cut into wedges; then, roll each wedge into a crescent.

Ginger-Nut Party Rounds

    1 cup all-purpose flour
    ¼ cup sugar
    ¼ teaspoon ground ginger
    6 tablespoons butter *or* margarine
    1 beaten egg yolk
    2½ tablespoons milk
    ¼ teaspoon vanilla
        • • •
    1 egg white
    2 tablespoons sugar
    2 tablespoons finely chopped nuts
        • • •
    2 tablespoons sugar
    ¼ teaspoon ground ginger

Stir together flour, ¼ cup sugar, and ¼ teaspoon ginger. With pastry blender, cut in butter till mixture resembles fine crumbs. Combine egg yolk, milk, and vanilla; blend into flour mixture. Cover; chill thoroughly.

Divide in half; keep chilled till ready to use. On lightly floured surface, roll *each* half of dough to ⅛-inch thickness. Cut with 2-inch round cookie cutter. Place on ungreased cookie sheet. Beat egg white till soft peaks form; gradually add 2 tablespoons sugar, beating till stiff but not dry. Fold in nuts. Spread a little of the meringue atop each cookie. Combine 2 tablespoons sugar and ¼ teaspoon ginger. Sprinkle over cookies. Bake at 350° for 12 to 14 minutes. Remove from pan; place on cooling rack. Repeat with remaining dough and meringue. Makes about 2½ dozen.

Sour Cream Pastries

    1 cup butter *or* margarine
    2 cups all-purpose flour
    1 beaten egg yolk
    ½ cup dairy sour cream
    ½ cup apricot preserves
    ½ cup flaked coconut
    ¼ cup finely chopped pecans
      Granulated sugar

With pastry blender cut butter into flour till mixture resembles fine crumbs. Combine egg yolk and sour cream; blend into flour mixture. Cover; chill several hours or overnight.

Divide dough into four equal portions; keep chilled till ready to use. On lightly floured surface, roll *each* portion to 10-inch circle. Spread with *2 tablespoons* of the preserves; sprinkle with *2 tablespoons* of the coconut and 1 *tablespoon* of the nuts.

With fluted pastry wheel, cut each circle into 12 wedges. Beginning at wide end of wedge, roll toward point. Sprinkle with a little sugar; place on ungreased cookie sheet. Bake at 350° till lightly browned, about 20 minutes. Remove to cooling rack. Makes 4 dozen.

Peanut Butter Cut-Outs

    ½ cup shortening
    ½ cup peanut butter
    ½ cup packed brown sugar
    ½ cup granulated sugar
    1 egg
    2 teaspoons shredded orange peel
      (optional)
    ¼ cup orange juice *or* milk
    1½ cups all-purpose flour
    ¾ teaspoon baking soda
    ¼ teaspoon salt

Cream shortening, peanut butter, and sugars. Blend in egg, peel, and juice or milk; mix well. Stir together flour, soda, and salt; stir into creamed mixture. Cover and chill 2 to 3 hours.

On lightly floured surface, roll chilled dough to ⅛-inch thickness; cut into desired shapes with assorted cookie cutters. Place on greased cookie sheet. Bake at 350° for 8 to 10 minutes. Cool on rack. Makes 4 dozen.

Anise Cut-Outs

Use candy to decorate these licorice-flavored treats for children at Halloween —

½ cup butter *or* margarine, softened
¾ cup sugar
1 egg
¼ cup molasses
2 cups all-purpose flour
2 teaspoons aniseed, crushed
¼ teaspoon baking soda
¼ teaspoon baking powder
⅛ teaspoon salt

Cream butter and sugar till light and fluffy; blend in egg and molasses. Thoroughly stir together flour, aniseed, baking soda, baking powder, and salt; stir into creamed mixture. Cover dough and chill 3 to 4 hours.

On lightly floured surface, roll chilled dough to ¼-inch thickness. Cut into desired shapes with assorted cookie cutters. Place on greased cookie sheet. Bake at 350° for 6 to 8 minutes. Cool on rack. Makes about 3 dozen.

Sherry-Almond Rounds

See footnote on page 25 for toasting nuts —

½ cup butter *or* margarine, softened
1 cup sifted powdered sugar
½ teaspoon vanilla
3 tablespoons sherry
1½ cups all-purpose flour
¼ teaspoon salt
½ cup finely chopped almonds, toasted
1 slightly beaten egg
2 tablespoons water
Red and green sugar crystals

Cream butter, powdered sugar, and vanilla. Stir in sherry. Stir together flour and salt; blend with creamed mixture. Stir in nuts.

Flatten dough between two sheets of waxed paper; roll to about ¼-inch thickness. Remove top sheet of paper; cut dough with scalloped round cookie cutter. Remove from paper to ungreased cookie sheet. Combine egg and water and brush lightly over cookies. Sprinkle with red and green sugar crystals. Bake at 375° till lightly browned, 12 to 14 minutes. Makes about 3 dozen cookies.

Coconut-Sugar Cookies

¾ cup butter *or* margarine, softened
⅔ cup granulated sugar
2 eggs
½ teaspoon almond extract
1¾ cups all-purpose flour
1½ teaspoons baking powder
¼ teaspoon salt
1 cup cookie coconut *or* finely chopped flaked coconut
• • •
3 tablespoons butter *or* margarine, softened
2 cups sifted powdered sugar
3 tablespoons milk
¼ teaspoon vanilla
Few drops almond extract

Cream together ¾ cup butter or margarine and granulated sugar till fluffy; blend in eggs, one at a time, beating well after each. Add ½ teaspoon almond extract. Thoroughly stir together flour, baking powder, and salt; stir into creamed mixture. Blend in coconut. Cover dough and chill for 2 to 3 hours.

On lightly floured surface, roll dough to ¼-inch thickness. Cut into desired shapes with assorted cookie cutters. Place on ungreased cookie sheet. Bake at 375° about 8 minutes.

In small mixing bowl cream together 3 tablespoons butter or margarine and powdered sugar. Blend in milk, vanilla, and a few drops almond extract. Spread frosting over cooled cookies. Makes about 3 dozen.

TEST KITCHEN TIP

Use a small pastry brush to spread egg glaze over *Sherry-Almond Rounds.* For added decoration, top cookies with colored sugar crystals before baking.

TEST KITCHEN TIP

To cut rolled cookie dough into diamonds, make parallel cuts lengthwise of rolled dough. Then, make diagonal cuts across the dough. Reroll scraps; repeat.

Date-Filled Sugar Cookies

    2 cups snipped pitted dates
    ½ cup water
    ⅓ cup granulated sugar
    2 tablespoons lemon juice
    ¼ teaspoon salt
    1 cup shortening
    ½ cup granulated sugar
    ½ cup packed brown sugar
    1 egg
    3 tablespoons milk
    1 teaspoon vanilla
    3 cups all-purpose flour
    ½ teaspoon baking soda
    ½ teaspoon salt

In saucepan combine dates, water, and ⅓ cup granulated sugar; bring to boil. Simmer, covered, about 5 minutes; stir occasionally. Add lemon juice and ¼ teaspoon salt. Cool.

Cream shortening and next 2 ingredients. Add egg, milk, and vanilla; beat well. Stir together flour, soda, and ½ teaspoon salt; add to creamed mixture. Mix well. Cover; chill 1 hour. Divide dough in half. On floured surface, roll *each* portion to ⅛-inch thickness. Cut into 2½-inch rounds with cookie cutter. Top *half* of the rounds with *scant tablespoon* cooled date mixture. With tiny cutter or thimble, cut small hole in center of remaining rounds. Place on date-topped rounds; seal edges of cookie with inverted teaspoon tip. Place 1 inch apart on ungreased cookie sheet. Bake at 350° for 10 to 12 minutes. Makes 30.

Spiced Diamonds

    1 cup butter *or* margarine, softened
    1 cup granulated sugar
    2 eggs
    1 tablespoon molasses
    2 teaspoons grated orange peel
        or grated lemon peel
    3 cups all-purpose flour
    1 teaspoon baking soda
    1 teaspoon ground cinnamon
    1 teaspoon ground ginger
    1 teaspoon ground nutmeg
    ½ teaspoon salt
    ½ teaspoon ground cardamom
    ½ teaspoon ground cloves
        • • •
    4 cups sifted powdered sugar
    ½ cup milk

In large bowl cream butter and granulated sugar. Add eggs, molasses, and peel; beat well. Stir flour with next 7 ingredients; add to creamed mixture. Mix well. Cover; chill.

Divide dough in fourths. On lightly floured surface, roll *each* portion to ⅛-inch thickness. With knife, cut into diamonds. Place on ungreased cookie sheet. Bake at 350° till edges are lightly browned, 8 to 10 minutes.

Mix powdered sugar and milk; add more milk, if needed, till of spreading consistency. Frost cooled cookies. Makes about 10 dozen.

Viennese Butter Rounds

Stir together 1 cup all-purpose flour, ½ cup ground pecans, and ⅓ cup granulated sugar. With spoon, blend in ½ cup softened butter *or* margarine. On floured surface, roll to 1/16-inch thickness. Cut into 1¾-inch rounds with cookie cutter. Place on ungreased cookie sheet. Bake at 375° till lightly browned, 5 to 6 minutes. Cool slightly; remove to rack.

Cream ¼ cup softened butter, ⅔ cup sifted powdered sugar, and one 1-ounce square unsweetened chocolate, melted and cooled. Spread mixture on bottoms of *half* the cookies. Spread bottoms of remaining cookies with ¼ cup apricot preserves. Assemble cookies sandwich-style, pressing the two types of fillings together. Sift powdered sugar over tops. Makes 24.

Rolled Sugar Cookies

Thin cookies are more crisp than thick ones—

> ½ **cup butter** *or* **margarine, softened**
> 1 **cup sugar**
> 1 **egg**
> ¼ **cup milk**
> ½ **teaspoon vanilla**
> 2¼ **cups all-purpose flour**
> 2 **teaspoons baking powder**
> ½ **teaspoon ground mace (optional)**

Cream butter and sugar. Add egg, milk, and vanilla; beat well. Stir flour with baking powder, mace, and ½ teaspoon salt; blend into creamed mixture. Divide in half. Cover; chill 1 hour. On lightly floured surface, roll *each* half to ⅛-inch thickness for thin cookies, or ¼-inch thickness for thick cookies. Cut into desired shapes with cookie cutters. Place on ungreased cookie sheet. Bake thin cookies at 375° for 7 to 8 minutes; bake thick cookies for 10 to 12 minutes. Makes 4 to 4½ dozen thin cookies *or* 3 dozen thick cookies.

Jam-Filled Cookies

> 1 **cup shortening**
> 1 **cup granulated sugar**
> 1 **cup packed brown sugar**
> 2 **eggs**
> ¼ **cup sour milk** *or* **buttermilk**
> 1 **teaspoon vanilla**
> 3½ **cups all-purpose flour**
> 1 **teaspoon baking powder**
> 1 **teaspoon baking soda**
> 1 **teaspoon salt**
> 1 **teaspoon ground nutmeg**
> **Strawberry preserves**

In large bowl cream shortening and sugars. Add eggs, milk, and vanilla; mix till smooth. Stir together flour and next 4 ingredients; stir into creamed mixture. Cover and chill.

On floured surface, roll to ⅛-inch thickness. Cut into 1½-inch rounds with cookie cutter. Place *1 teaspoon* preserves on *half* of the rounds; top with remaining rounds. Lightly seal edges with fork. With knife, cut crisscross slits in tops of cookies. Bake at 350° till golden, 10 to 15 minutes. Makes 5 dozen.

Grandmother's Jelly Cookies

These cookies are shown on pages 34 and 35—

> 1 **cup butter** *or* **margarine, softened**
> 1 **cup sugar**
> 1 **egg**
> 3 **cups all-purpose flour**
> ½ **teaspoon salt**
> 1 **slightly beaten egg white**
> ½ **cup finely chopped almonds**
> ½ **cup red currant jelly**

Have ready one 2½-inch round cutter, one 2-inch scalloped round cutter, and a thimble.

Cream butter and ¾ *cup* of the sugar; beat in egg. Combine flour and salt; add to batter. Mix well. Roll on floured surface to ⅛-inch thickness. Cut into at least fifty-four 2½-inch rounds with cutter. (Reroll as needed.) Bake *36* of the rounds on ungreased cookie sheet at 375° for 8 to 10 minutes.

Center scalloped cutter on unbaked rounds; cut dough. (You now have scalloped rounds and cut-out rims.) Using thimble, cut centers out of scalloped rounds. Carefully place all cut-outs (scalloped rounds, cut-out rims, and thimble-cut pieces) on ungreased cookie sheet. Brush with egg white; sprinkle with nuts and remaining sugar. Bake at 375° for 6 to 8 minutes. To assemble cookies, spread jelly on top of large plain rounds. Place scalloped rounds atop the jelly on *half* of the cookies, nut side up. On remaining jelly-spread cookies, place a cut-out rim. Then place a thimble-cut piece in center. Makes 3 dozen.

TEST KITCHEN TIP

With sharp knife, cut shallow crisscross slits in *Jam-Filled Cookies* to allow steam to escape during baking. Cut carefully to avoid cutting through bottom of cookies.

Sprightly Shaped Cookies

Finnish Chestnut Fingers

   6 tablespoons butter *or* margarine,
       softened
   ¼ cup sugar
   1 egg yolk
   ½ cup chestnut purée *or* canned
       chestnuts, drained and pureed
   ¼ teaspoon vanilla
   1 cup all-purpose flour
   ¼ teaspoon salt
   ¼ teaspoon ground cinnamon
   1 slightly beaten egg white
       Sugar
   ½ cup semisweet chocolate pieces,
       melted

Cream butter and ¼ cup sugar; add egg yolk. Beat till light and fluffy. Beat in purée and vanilla. Stir together flour, salt, and cinnamon; stir into creamed mixture.

Using a scant tablespoon dough for each cookie, roll into 2½-inch fingers. Dip one side of each finger in egg white, then in sugar. Place sugar-side-up on greased cookie sheet. Bake at 350° till slightly browned, about 20 minutes. Remove from pan; cool on rack. Dip one end of each cookie in chocolate; place on waxed paper till set. Makes 2½ dozen.

Berlinerkranser

In bowl cream together 1 cup softened butter *or* margarine and ½ cup sifted powdered sugar. Add 1 hard-cooked egg yolk, sieved; 1 raw egg yolk; and 1 teaspoon vanilla. Stir in 2¼ cups all-purpose flour. Cover and chill.

Work with a small amount of dough at a time; keep remainder chilled. Break off walnut-sized pieces of dough. With hands, roll each piece to about a 6-inch rope, ½ inch in diameter. Shape into a wreath, overlapping about 1 inch from ends. Place on ungreased cookie sheet. Brush with 1 slightly beaten egg white; sprinkle with crushed sugar cubes. Bake at 350° about 12 minutes. Makes 3½ dozen.

Brown Sugar Spritz

   Holiday Pineapple Filling
   1 cup butter *or* margarine, softened
   ½ cup packed brown sugar
   1 egg
   1 teaspoon vanilla
   2⅔ cups all-purpose flour
   1 teaspoon baking powder

Prepare Holiday Pineapple Filling; cool. Cream together butter and brown sugar; beat in egg and vanilla. Stir together flour and baking powder; add gradually to creamed mixture, mixing till smooth. Do not chill.

Place *half* of dough in cookie press.* Using ribbon plate, press dough in ten 10-inch strips on ungreased cookie sheets. Using star plate and remaining dough, press lengthwise rows of dough on top of each strip, making a rim along both edges. Spoon red or green Holiday Pineapple Filling between rims atop ribbon strips. Bake cookies at 400° for 8 to 10 minutes. While hot, cut strips into 1¼-inch diagonals. Cool. Makes about 6½ dozen.

Holiday Pineapple Filling: In saucepan stir together one 29½-ounce can crushed pineapple, drained, and 1 cup granulated sugar; bring to boiling. Simmer till mixture is very thick, 30 to 35 minutes, stirring often. Divide fruit filling in half. Using a few drops food coloring, tint half of the filling red and the other half green. Cool thoroughly.

Note: Or, omit Filling and force all of dough through cookie press on ungreased cookie sheet into desired shapes. Shake ground almonds with a few drops red *or* green food coloring in screw-top jar; sprinkle over cookies. Bake at 400° for 8 minutes. Makes about 60.

Rich in heritage as well as design are wreath-shaped Norwegian *Berlinerkranser*, chocolate-dipped *Finnish Chestnut Fingers*, and German *Brown Sugar Spritz* topped with a bright-colored pineapple filling or tinted almonds.

TEST KITCHEN TIP

To make uniform ribbon strips in *Candy Bar Cushions*, hold cookie press at a 45° angle over cookie sheet. Carry dough evenly across pan using long movements.

Peanut Butter Press Cookies

½ cup creamy peanut butter
¼ cup butter *or* margarine, softened
½ cup granulated sugar
½ cup packed brown sugar
1 egg
¾ cup all-purpose flour
1 teaspoon baking soda

Cream first 4 ingredients; beat in egg. Stir together flour, soda, and dash salt; add to creamed mixture. Mix well. Chill 10 minutes. Using *half* the dough at a time, force through cookie press on ungreased cookie sheet. If desired, sprinkle with finely chopped peanuts. Bake at 400° about 8 minutes. Makes 5 dozen.

Nut Crescents

Rich, dainty cookies shown on pages 82 and 83—

1 cup butter *or* margarine, softened
⅓ cup granulated sugar
1 teaspoon vanilla
2 cups all-purpose flour
½ cup chopped salted peanuts, pecans, toasted almonds, *or* walnuts
Sifted powdered sugar

Cream first 3 ingredients and 1 tablespoon water. Stir in flour and nuts; mix well. Shape into crescents. Place on ungreased cookie sheet. Bake at 350° for 15 to 20 minutes. Cool on rack; roll in powdered sugar. Makes 60.

Candy Bar Cushions

Cookie strips break apart easily after baking—

1 cup butter *or* margarine, softened
⅔ cup sugar
1 egg
1 teaspoon vanilla
2½ cups all-purpose flour
9 ⅝-ounce bars milk chocolate

Cream butter and sugar till fluffy. Beat in egg and vanilla. Stir in flour. Place *half* of the dough in cookie press. Using ribbon plate, press strips on ungreased cookie sheets.

Break candy bars into squares; place candy pieces ½ inch apart atop dough strips. Lightly press candy into dough. Force remaining dough through press in strips over candy. Mark between candy pieces with table knife. Bake at 375° for 12 to 13 minutes. Immediately cut into cookies where marked. Makes 4½ dozen.

Apricot-Chocolate Spritz

¾ cup butter *or* margarine, softened
½ cup sugar
1 egg
2 1-ounce squares unsweetened chocolate, melted and cooled
2¼ cups all-purpose flour
½ teaspoon salt
1 teaspoon almond extract
• • •
½ cup apricot preserves, sieved
½ cup chopped almonds
2 tablespoons sugar

Cream together butter and ½ cup sugar. Add egg; beat well. Stir in cooled chocolate. Stir together flour and salt; add to creamed mixture with almond extract. Mix well.

Place *half* of the dough in cookie press. Using ribbon plate, make four strips 12½ inches long on ungreased cookie sheet. Spread *each* strip with about *2 teaspoons* of the preserves. Press another strip of dough over filling. Combine almonds and 2 tablespoons sugar; sprinkle *half* of the mixture over strips. Cut into 2½-inch bars. Make additional cookies with remaining dough, preserves, and nut mixture. Bake at 400° for 12 minutes. Makes 40.

Double Peanut Cookies

> 1 cup shortening
> 1 cup peanut butter
> 1 cup granulated sugar
> 1 cup packed brown sugar
> 2 eggs
> 1 teaspoon vanilla
> 2¼ cups all-purpose flour
> 2 teaspoons baking soda
> 1 cup coarsely chopped salted peanuts

Cream first 4 ingredients; beat in eggs and vanilla. Stir together flour, soda, and ¼ teaspoon salt; blend into batter. Stir in nuts. Form into 1-inch balls. Place on ungreased cookie sheet; flatten slightly with fingers. Bake at 350° for 10 minutes. Makes 6 dozen.

Butter Pecan Cookies

These melt-in-your-mouth cookies are pictured as a gift suggestion on pages 82 and 83—

> 1 cup butter *or* margarine, softened
> ⅔ cup packed brown sugar
> 1 egg
> 2 cups all-purpose flour
> Pecan halves

Cream butter and sugar; blend in egg. Stir together flour and ½ teaspoon salt; stir into creamed mixture. Chill 1 hour. Form into 1-inch balls; place 2 inches apart on ungreased cookie sheet. Flatten in one direction with fork tines; top each with a pecan half. Bake at 375° for 10 to 12 minutes. Makes 4 dozen.

Gingersnaps

Combine 1 cup packed brown sugar, ¾ cup cooking oil, ¼ cup dark molasses, and 1 egg; beat well. Stir together 2 cups all-purpose flour, 2 teaspoons baking soda, 1 teaspoon ground cinnamon, 1 teaspoon ground ginger, ½ teaspoon ground cloves, and ¼ teaspoon salt. Gradually blend into molasses mixture. Using about 1 tablespoon for each, form into 1¼-inch balls. Roll in granulated sugar; place 2 inches apart on greased cookie sheet. Bake at 375° for 10 to 12 minutes. Makes 4 dozen.

Sweet Chocolate Cookies

These fudge-rich cookies are shown on page 89—

Cream 1 cup softened butter *or* margarine and 1⅓ cups sifted powdered sugar. Beat in 2 tablespoons water and 1 teaspoon vanilla. Add two 4-ounce packages sweet cooking chocolate, grated (2 cups); 2 cups all-purpose flour; and dash salt. Mix well. Stir in ½ cup finely chopped walnuts. Form into 1-inch balls; place on ungreased cookie sheet. Bake at 325° about 25 minutes. Cool. If desired, sift powdered sugar over tops. Makes 6 dozen.

Mocha Logs

> 1 cup butter *or* margarine, softened
> ¾ cup sugar
> 1 egg
> 1 teaspoon vanilla
> 2¼ cups all-purpose flour
> 2 tablespoons instant coffee crystals
> ¼ teaspoon baking powder
> Semisweet chocolate, melted
> Finely chopped pecans

Cream butter and sugar; beat in egg and vanilla. Stir together flour, coffee, baking powder, and ½ teaspoon salt; slowly blend into creamed mixture. Using star plate, force through cookie press in 3-inch strips on ungreased cookie sheet. Bake at 375° for 10 to 12 minutes. Cool. Dip one end of each cookie in chocolate, then coat with nuts. Makes 6½ dozen.

TEST KITCHEN TIP

A quick and easy method for decorating finger-shaped cookies is to dip one end into melted chocolate, then coat with nuts. The chocolate will harden as it cools.

Oatmeal Cookies

1 cup all-purpose flour
½ cup granulated sugar
½ cup packed brown sugar
½ teaspoon baking powder
½ teaspoon baking soda
¼ teaspoon salt
½ cup shortening
1 egg
¼ teaspoon vanilla
¾ cup quick-cooking rolled oats
¼ cup chopped walnuts
    Granulated sugar

In mixing bowl stir together first 6 ingredients. Add shortening, egg, and vanilla; beat well. Stir in oats and nuts. Form into small balls. Dip tops in additional granulated sugar. Place on ungreased cookie sheet. Bake at 375° for 10 to 12 minutes. Makes 3½ dozen.

Chocolate-Oatmeal Cookies

A welcome gift idea as shown on pages 82 and 83—

½ cup shortening
1 cup sugar
1 egg
2 1-ounce squares unsweetened
    chocolate, melted and cooled
1 teaspoon vanilla
½ teaspoon rum flavoring
1 cup all-purpose flour
½ teaspoon baking soda
1 cup quick-cooking rolled oats
½ cup chopped pecans

Cream shortening and sugar; beat in egg. Blend in chocolate, flavorings, and 2 tablespoons water. Mix flour with soda and ½ teaspoon salt; stir into creamed mixture. Stir in oats and nuts. Form into 1-inch balls; place 2 inches apart on greased cookie sheet. Flatten with sugared bottom of tumbler. Bake at 350° for 10 to 12 minutes. Makes 4 dozen.

◀ **Golden brown** *Oatmeal Cookies* are crunchy on the outside, yet chewy in the center. Serve with an iced beverage for a cool summer snack.

Oatmeal Gingersnaps

1½ cups all-purpose flour
1 cup sugar
¾ cup quick-cooking rolled oats
1 teaspoon baking soda
1 teaspoon ground ginger
¼ teaspoon ground cloves
½ cup shortening
¼ cup molasses
1 egg
    Sugar

Stir together first 6 ingredients and ¼ teaspoon salt. Blend in shortening, molasses, and egg; beat well with electric mixer for 2 minutes. Form into 1-inch balls. Roll in sugar; place 2 inches apart on greased cookie sheet. Bake at 375° for 8 to 10 minutes. Let stand 1 minute; cool on rack. Makes 3½ dozen.

Ranger Cookies

Cream ½ cup softened butter *or* margarine, ½ cup packed brown sugar, and ½ cup granulated sugar. Add 1 egg and 1 teaspoon vanilla; beat well. Stir together 1¼ cups all-purpose flour, ½ teaspoon baking powder, ½ teaspoon baking soda, and ½ teaspoon salt; stir into creamed mixture. Stir in 2 cups crisp rice cereal, one 3½-ounce can flaked coconut (1⅓ cups), and 1 cup chopped pitted dates.

Form into ¾-inch balls; place 2½ inches apart on ungreased cookie sheet. Bake at 350° till lightly browned, about 10 minutes. Cool slightly; remove to rack. Makes 5 dozen.

Natural Grain Spice Cookies

Beat together ¾ cup light molasses, ½ cup cooking oil, ¼ cup sugar, and 1 egg. Stir together 2 cups rye flour, ¼ cup soy flour, ¼ cup whole wheat flour, 3 tablespoons nonfat dry milk powder, 1 teaspoon ground ginger, 1 teaspoon ground cinnamon, and ½ teaspoon salt. Add to molasses mixture; mix well. Chill. Form into 1-inch balls; roll in additional sugar. Place on greased cookie sheet; flatten with sugared bottom of tumbler. Bake at 350° for 10 to 12 minutes. Makes about 3 dozen.

TEST KITCHEN TIP

Shaping *Ladyfingers* presents no problems when specialty baking pans are not available. Simply pipe batter through a pastry bag using steady pressure.

Chocolate Pretzels

An unusual cookie shown on pages 34 and 35 —

½ **cup butter** *or* **margarine, softened**
½ **cup granulated sugar**
¼ **cup unsweetened cocoa powder**
1 **egg**
¼ **cup water**
1 **teaspoon vanilla**
2 **cups all-purpose flour**
2 **1-ounce squares semisweet chocolate**
2 **tablespoons butter** *or* **margarine**
2 **cups sifted powdered sugar**
1 **teaspoon vanilla**

Combine ½ cup butter, granulated sugar, and cocoa powder; beat in egg, water, and 1 teaspoon vanilla. Gradually add flour; mix well.

Divide dough into 24 pieces. With hands, roll each piece to a 12-inch rope on lightly floured surface. Shape each rope into a circle, crossing about 2 inches from ends of rope. Twist rope at point where rope crosses. Seal ends of rope to center of opposite side of circle, forming a pretzel shape. Place on ungreased cookie sheet. Bake at 350° for 10 minutes. Cool on rack.

In small saucepan melt chocolate and 2 tablespoons butter over low heat, stirring constantly; remove from heat. Stir in powdered sugar and 1 teaspoon vanilla. Blend in enough hot water till of glaze consistency. Working over frosting pan, spoon glaze over pretzels; dry on rack. (Add a little hot water to thin glaze, if needed.) Makes 2 dozen.

Ladyfingers

4 **egg whites**
½ **cup granulated sugar**
4 **egg yolks**
2 **teaspoons lemon juice**
1 **teaspoon vanilla**
¾ **cup sifted cake flour**
Powdered sugar

Beat egg whites and dash salt till soft peaks form; gradually add ¼ *cup* of the granulated sugar, beating till stiff but not dry.

In small mixing bowl beat yolks till fluffy. Gradually add remaining granulated sugar; beat till thick and lemon-colored. Beat in juice and vanilla. Fold yolks into whites; by hand, fold in flour. Line cookie sheet with plain brown paper. Insert straight-sided ½-inch round tip in pastry bag; fill with batter. Pipe 4x1-inch strips 1 inch apart on paper. Or, spoon into ungreased ladyfinger pans. Lightly sift powdered sugar over all. Bake at 350° for 8 to 10 minutes. Makes 20.

Chocolate Snapper Cookies

½ **cup butter** *or* **margarine, softened**
⅓ **cup granulated sugar**
1 **egg yolk**
1 **teaspoon vanilla**
¾ **cup all-purpose flour**
72 **pecan halves (⅔ cup)**
2 **tablespoons butter** *or* **margarine**
1 **1-ounce square unsweetened chocolate**
1 **cup sifted powdered sugar**
½ **teaspoon vanilla**
¼ **teaspoon salt**

Cream first 2 ingredients. Beat in egg yolk and 1 teaspoon vanilla. Add flour; mix well. Cover; chill. Shape dough into 24 balls. On ungreased cookie sheet, place *each* ball atop 3 pecans arranged to resemble turtle candies. Bake at 375° about 10 minutes. Carefully remove from pan to cooling rack.

Melt 2 tablespoons butter with chocolate over low heat; stir constantly. Remove from heat; stir in remaining ingredients. Add 2 tablespoons boiling water; beat smooth. Spread frosting atop cookies. Makes 2 dozen.

Snickerdoodles

If desired, dip bottom of tumbler in cinnamon-sugar to use in flattening balls of cookie dough—

> 1 cup butter *or* margarine, softened
> 2 cups sugar
> 2 eggs
> ¼ cup milk
> 1 teaspoon vanilla
> 3¾ cups all-purpose flour
> ½ teaspoon baking soda
> ½ teaspoon cream of tartar
> ½ teaspoon salt
> 1 cup chopped nuts

In mixing bowl cream butter or margarine and sugar till light and fluffy. Add eggs, one at a time, beating well after each. Blend in milk and vanilla. Thoroughly stir together flour, baking soda, cream of tartar, and salt; stir into creamed mixture. Blend in chopped nuts. Form dough into 1-inch balls. Place balls 2 inches apart on greased cookie sheet. Lightly flatten balls with sugared bottom of tumbler. Bake cookies at 375° till done, 10 to 12 minutes. Makes about 8 dozen.

Shaped Almond Cookies

See footnote on page 25 for toasting nuts—

> ¾ cup butter *or* margarine, softened
> ½ cup granulated sugar
> ¼ cup packed brown sugar
> 1 egg
> ½ teaspoon almond extract
> 2 cups all-purpose flour
> ½ teaspoon baking powder
> ½ teaspoon salt
> ½ cup finely chopped almonds, toasted
>   Whole blanched almonds, halved

In mixing bowl cream together butter, granulated sugar, and brown sugar till fluffy. Add egg and extract; beat well. Stir together flour, baking powder, and salt; gradually add to creamed mixture. Stir in chopped almonds. Form dough into 1-inch balls. Place on ungreased cookie sheet. If desired, flatten each ball to a 2-inch circle. Press an almond half atop each. Bake at 350° till lightly browned, 10 to 12 minutes. Makes about 4 dozen.

Almond Macaroons

Only 3 ingredients go into this chewy cookie—

In mixing bowl crumble one 8-ounce can almond paste (1 cup); gradually add 1 cup sugar. Add 2 egg whites to almond mixture; beat till smooth. (Dough will be stiff.)

Insert large star tube in pastry bag; fill with dough. Using a slight swirling motion, squeeze dough on well-greased cookie sheet; lift tube ¼ inch from pan till dough breaks easily. Or, drop dough from teaspoon on well-greased cookie sheet. Bake at 350° for 15 to 18 minutes. Immediately remove from pan; cool on rack. Makes about 3 dozen.

Fortune Cookies

Before you start, write fortunes on small strips of paper for enclosing in cookies—

Stir together ¼ cup sifted cake flour, 2 tablespoons sugar, 1 tablespoon cornstarch, and dash salt. Add 2 tablespoons cooking oil and 1 egg white; stir till mixture is smooth. Add 1 tablespoon water; mix thoroughly.

Make one cookie at a time. On lightly greased skillet or griddle, pour *1 tablespoon* of the batter; spread to 3½-inch circle. Cook over low heat till lightly browned, about 4 minutes. Turn with wide spatula; cook 1 minute more. Working quickly, place cookie on pot holder; put fortune in center. Fold cookie in half, then fold again over edge of bowl. Place cookies in muffin pan to cool. Makes 8.

TEST KITCHEN TIP

Fold skillet-baked *Fortune Cookies* in half, then fold again over edge of a bowl to make characteristic cookie shape. Place folded cookies in muffin pan to cool.

Special-Day Cookies

The best remembered holidays and parties undoubtedly include cookies especially made for red-letter days. They're as much a part of the festive foods as eggnog at a Christmas caroling party and punch at an afternoon tea.

The cookies in the holiday section go hand-in-hand with Christmas. Not only do they look beautiful, but they taste great. So, when visions of sugar plums dance in your head, look here for many old-time cookie favorites and new-fangled Yuletide goodies, too. Many of the traditional cookies are specialties from other countries adapted to fit American tastes.

At teas and coffees, cookies are a must, too, because they're easy to eat regardless of whether guests are standing or sitting. Make the cookies party-fancy by shaping them creatively. The conversation will focus quickly on food if you use the recipes in this section.

Extra-fancy cookies included here are (clockwise, starting at top): *Chocolate Waffle Drops, Vanilla Waffle Drops, Black-Eyed Susans, Krumkake,* and *Candy Cane Cookies.* (See Index for page numbers.)

Holiday Favorites

Spritz

If desired, tint dough with food coloring—

> 1 cup butter *or* margarine, softened
> 1 cup sugar
> 1 egg
> 1 teaspoon vanilla *or* ½ teaspoon
>   almond extract
> 2⅓ cups all-purpose flour
> ½ teaspoon baking powder
> ¼ teaspoon salt

Cream butter and sugar; blend in egg and flavoring. Combine dry ingredients; stir into creamed mixture. Mix well. Do *not* chill the dough. Pack dough, *half* at a time, in cookie press. Press into desired shapes on ungreased cookie sheet. If desired, sprinkle with colored sugar crystals or trim with pieces of red and green candied cherries, pressing cherries lightly into dough. Bake at 400° for 7 to 8 minutes. Cool. Makes about 6 dozen.

Rosettes

> 2 eggs
> 1 tablespoon granulated sugar
> 1 cup all-purpose flour
> 1 cup milk
> 1 teaspoon vanilla
> Fat for frying
> Powdered sugar

Combine eggs, granulated sugar, and ¼ teaspoon salt; beat well. Add flour, milk, and vanilla; beat smooth. Heat rosette iron in deep hot fat (375°). Dip hot iron in batter, being careful batter comes only ¾ of the way up side of iron. Fry rosette in deep hot fat till golden, about ½ minute. Lift iron out of fat; tip slightly to drain. With fork, push rosette off iron onto paper toweling placed on rack. Continue making rosettes with remaining batter, being certain iron is reheated each time before dipping in batter. Sift powdered sugar over cooled rosettes. Makes 3½ dozen.

Pepparkakor

Let children help you cut and decorate these Swedish rolled ginger cookies—

> 1 cup shortening
> 1 cup granulated sugar
> 1 cup molasses
> 1 egg
> 2 tablespoons vinegar
> 5 cups all-purpose flour
> 2 to 3 teaspoons ground ginger
> 1½ teaspoons baking soda
> 1 teaspoon ground cinnamon
> 1 teaspoon ground cloves
> ½ teaspoon salt
> • • •
> ½ cup shortening
> 1 teaspoon vanilla
> 1 pound sifted powdered sugar
>   (3 to 4 cups)
> 3 to 4 tablespoons milk

Cream 1 cup shortening and granulated sugar. Beat in molasses, egg, and vinegar. Stir flour with ginger, soda, cinnamon, cloves, and salt; blend into batter. Chill 3 hours.

On lightly floured surface, roll dough to ⅛-inch thickness. Cut into desired shapes with assorted cookie cutters. Place 1 inch apart on greased cookie sheet. Bake at 375° for 5 to 6 minutes. Cool slightly; remove cookies to rack and cool thoroughly.

Meanwhile, blend ½ cup shortening and vanilla with electric mixer. Gradually add powdered sugar; beat just till combined. Stir in milk. Insert small plain tip in pastry bag or cake decorator; fill with frosting. To decorate cookies, pipe frosting in straight or wavy lines, as desired. Makes about 5 dozen.

Liven the holiday season with a cookie smorgasbord for friends after an evening of caroling. Offer an assortment of Scandinavian favorites, such as buttery *Spritz*, sugar-coated *Rosettes*, and spicy *Pepparkakor* decorated with icing.

TEST KITCHEN TIP

To shape *Konjakskransar*, roll dough into pencil-like ropes. Carefully twist two of the ropes together, then form into a ring. Pinch ends of ring together to seal.

Konjakskransar

Mix 2½ cups all-purpose flour, 1 cup butter *or* margarine, ½ cup sugar, and 3 tablespoons apricot brandy. Work with hands to a soft dough. Do not chill. Using a rounded teaspoon of dough for each, roll with hands to 5-inch ropes on lightly floured surface. Twist 2 ropes together; shape into a ring. Seal ends together. Place on greased cookie sheet. Bake at 350° for 13 to 15 minutes. Makes 3 dozen.

Florentines

See footnote on page 25 for toasting almonds —

   ¼ **cup butter** *or* **margarine**
   ⅓ **cup packed brown sugar**
   ¼ **cup light cream**
   ¼ **cup all-purpose flour**
   ¾ **cup finely chopped almonds, toasted**
   ½ **cup candied orange peel, finely
       chopped**
   1 **4-ounce package sweet cooking
       chocolate, melted**

Melt butter; remove from heat. Stir in sugar and cream. Add flour and dash salt; blend till smooth. Stir in nuts and peel. Drop level tablespoonfuls 3 inches apart on greased cookie sheet. Flatten slightly with back of spoon. Bake at 350° for 8 minutes. Let stand 1 minute; cool on rack. Invert cookies; spread chocolate over bottoms. When set, store right side up in refrigerator. Makes 20.

Uppakrakakor

   1 **cup butter** *or* **margarine, softened**
   ¾ **cup sifted powdered sugar**
   1 **teaspoon vanilla**
   1¾ **cups all-purpose flour**
   ½ **cup cornstarch**
   1 **slightly beaten egg** *or* **¼ cup milk**
   ½ **cup finely chopped almonds**
   2 **teaspoons granulated sugar**

Cream butter, powdered sugar, and vanilla. Stir flour with cornstarch; add to creamed mixture. Blend well. Cover; chill 30 minutes.

Divide dough in fourths. Keep remaining chilled till ready to use. On floured surface, roll *each* portion to ⅛-inch thickness; cut into 2-inch rounds with cookie cutter. Cut *each* round in half, slightly off center. Stack smaller part atop larger part, cut sides together. Place on ungreased cookie sheet. Brush with egg or milk; sprinkle with nuts and granulated sugar. Bake at 350° till golden, about 10 minutes. Makes 4½ dozen.

Ragkakor

A Swedish cookie made with dark flours —

   ½ **cup butter** *or* **margarine, softened**
   ⅓ **cup sugar**
   ½ **cup all-purpose flour**
   ½ **cup rye flour**
   ½ **cup whole wheat flour**
   ¼ **teaspoon baking powder**
   ¼ **teaspoon salt**
   2 **to 3 tablespoons cold water**

Cream butter and sugar till fluffy. Stir together flours, baking powder, and salt; stir into creamed mixture. Gradually add cold water, mixing just till all is moistened. Form into a ball. On lightly floured surface, roll dough to ⅛-inch thickness. Cut into 2½-inch rounds with cookie cutter.* Using a thimble or ½-inch round cutter, cut a circle out of *each* round. Place cookies on ungreased cookie sheet. Bake at 375° till lightly browned, 10 to 12 minutes. Cool slightly; remove cookies to rack. Makes 3 to 4 dozen.

*Or, cut into 1½-inch squares with pastry wheel. Omit cutting circle out of cookies.

Pfeffernuesse

⅓ **cup dark corn syrup**
¼ **cup honey**
¼ **cup sugar**
¼ **cup shortening**
1 **beaten egg**
2¼ **cups all-purpose flour**
½ **teaspoon baking soda**
¼ **teaspoon** *each* **ground cloves, ground allspice, and ground cinnamon**

Combine first 4 ingredients; cook and stir till shortening and sugar melt. Cool. Stir in egg. Mix flour with soda and spices. Add to honey mixture; mix well. Form into balls using one level tablespoon of dough for each; place on greased cookie sheet. Bake at 375° about 10 minutes. Cool. If desired, sift powdered sugar over tops. Makes 4 to 4½ dozen.

Holiday Peppernuts

⅓ **cup packed brown sugar**
⅓ **cup dark corn syrup**
2 **tablespoons milk**
2 **tablespoons shortening** *or* **lard**
1 **egg**
½ **teaspoon anise extract**
¼ **teaspoon baking powder**
¼ **teaspoon vanilla**
⅛ **teaspoon ground cloves**
⅛ **teaspoon ground cardamom**
2½ **cups all-purpose flour**
Powdered sugar

Combine brown sugar, corn syrup, milk, and shortening; heat to boiling. Cool. Beat in egg. Add extract, next 4 ingredients, ⅛ teaspoon salt, and dash black pepper; mix well. Mix in enough flour to make a very stiff dough, kneading in the last addition.

On surface dusted with powdered sugar, shape dough into ropes ⅜- to ¾-inch in diameter. Cut ropes in ⅜- to ¾-inch lengths. Place on ungreased cookie sheet. Bake at 375° till browned, 8 to 12 minutes. Cool 1 to 2 minutes; remove to rack. Cookies will harden upon standing. Store larger cookies in airtight container with apple slice. Makes 32 dozen ⅜-inch or 8 dozen ¾-inch cookies.

Letterbanket

Inspired by the Dutch, these St. Nicholas' Eve letter-shaped cookies are almond-filled—

Combine one 8-ounce can almond paste (1 cup), 1 egg, and ¼ cup sugar; mix well. Chill.

Stir together 3 cups all-purpose flour and ¾ teaspoon salt. Cut in 1½ cups butter *or* margarine till mixture resembles coarse crumbs. Add ½ to ⅔ cup ice water, a tablespoon at a time, till dough is moistened. Shape into a ball; cover. Let stand 30 minutes.

Divide dough in thirds. On lightly floured surface, roll one part to 12x6-inch rectangle. Cut in half lengthwise, forming two 12x3-inch strips. For *each* strip, roll *3 tablespoons* of the almond filling to an 11-inch log on very lightly floured surface. Place a log in center of each strip. Moisten edges of dough with a small amount of water. Fold dough over filling; seal side seam and ends. Place long rolls on ungreased cookie sheet.

Roll *each* of the remaining parts of dough to an 8-inch square. Cut each square into four 8x2-inch strips. For *each* strip, roll *about 1 tablespoon* of the filling to an 8-inch log. Place a log on each strip; moisten and seal as for long rolls. Shape into desired letters. Place on ungreased cookie sheets.

Combine 1 egg yolk and 1 tablespoon water; brush on letters and long rolls. Bake at 375° till done, 30 to 35 minutes for letters and 40 to 45 minutes for long rolls. Cool. Cut long rolls into 1-inch pieces. Makes 2 long rolls and 8 individual letters.

TEST KITCHEN TIP

To enclose almond filling in *Letterbanket*, place filling log in center of dough strip. Moisten edges of dough, then carefully wrap dough over log; seal side and ends.

Honey Macaroonies

1½ cups quick-cooking rolled oats
½ cup flaked coconut
½ cup chopped walnuts
½ cup all-purpose flour
• • •
¾ cup packed brown sugar
½ cup butter *or* margarine
2 tablespoons honey
36 red *or* green candied cherries

In large mixing bowl stir together rolled oats, flaked coconut, chopped walnuts, and flour; set aside. In saucepan combine brown sugar, butter or margarine, and honey; bring mixture to boiling, stirring frequently. Pour over oat mixture, blending well.

For each cookie, press one level tablespoonful mixture into greased 1¾-inch muffin pan. (For flatter, crisper cookie, place in 2-inch muffin pan.) Top each cookie with a candied cherry. Bake at 350° till well browned, 15 to 20 minutes. Cool 10 minutes in pan; remove to rack. Cool thoroughly. Makes 3 dozen.

Chocolate-Rum Balls

Use blender to crush chocolate wafers —

1½ cups finely crushed chocolate wafers
    (30 wafers)
½ cup sifted powdered sugar
½ cup finely chopped walnuts
¼ cup light corn syrup
3 tablespoons rum
½ teaspoon shredded orange peel
¼ cup sifted powdered sugar

In bowl stir together chocolate wafers, ½ cup powdered sugar, and finely chopped nuts. Stir in light corn syrup, rum, and shredded orange peel. Using one level tablespoonful for each cookie, shape mixture into ¾-inch balls. Roll in ¼ cup powdered sugar. Store in covered container. Makes 2 to 2½ dozen.

◀ **Tote cherry-topped** *Honey Macaroonies* to friends in colorful, hand-crafted clay boxes. (See directions for making boxes on page 89.)

Filbert Balls

Filbert fans will relish these sweet morsels —

1 cup butter *or* margarine, softened
½ cup sifted powdered sugar
2 tablespoons water
1 teaspoon vanilla
2 cups all-purpose flour
1 cup chopped filberts
    Powdered sugar

In mixing bowl cream butter or margarine and ½ cup powdered sugar till light and fluffy; blend in water and vanilla. Stir in flour and chopped filberts. For easier handling, cover dough and chill about 30 minutes.

Shape into 1-inch balls; place on ungreased cookie sheet. Bake at 350° for 12 to 15 minutes. Cool slightly; sift powdered sugar over cookies. Makes about 4 dozen.

Yuletide Drops

Rich with pecans, dates, raisins, and cherries —

½ cup butter *or* margarine, softened
1 cup sugar
2 eggs
¼ cup dairy sour cream
1¼ cups all-purpose flour
½ teaspoon baking soda
½ teaspoon ground cinnamon
¼ teaspoon salt
¼ teaspoon ground cloves
1 cup quick-cooking rolled oats
1 cup chopped pecans
1 cup finely snipped pitted dates
½ cup raisins
½ cup chopped candied cherries
    Halved candied cherries

Cream together butter or margarine, sugar, and eggs till fluffy; blend in sour cream. Stir together flour, baking soda, cinnamon, salt, and cloves; stir into creamed mixture. Stir in oats, chopped pecans, snipped dates, raisins, and chopped candied cherries.

Drop rounded teaspoonfuls 2 inches apart on lightly greased cookie sheet. Top each cookie with a candied cherry half. Bake at 350° for 10 to 12 minutes. Remove cookies from pan; cool on rack. Makes 5 dozen.

Festive Tassies

½ cup butter *or* margarine, softened
1 3-ounce package cream cheese,
　softened
1 cup all-purpose flour
　Lemon Curd Filling, Pumpkin Filling,
　Pecan Filling, Almond Filling, *or*
　Fruit Filling

Blend butter and cream cheese together; stir in flour. Cover; chill 1 hour. On lightly floured surface, roll to ⅛-inch thickness.* Cut in 3-inch rounds with scalloped cookie cutter. Pat rounds in 1¾-inch muffin pans. Bake according to filling directions. Makes 24.

*Or, divide dough into 24 balls. Place in 1¾-inch muffin pans and press evenly against bottom and sides of muffin cups.

Lemon Curd Filling: Bake tart shells at 400° for 10 to 12 minutes. Cool in pans. Grate ½ teaspoon lemon peel; set aside. In saucepan combine 3 well-beaten eggs, 1¼ cups sugar, ⅓ cup lemon juice, and ¼ cup butter *or* margarine. Cook and stir over low heat till thick, about 15 minutes. Remove from heat; stir in lemon peel. Chill. Spoon a rounded teaspoonful of filling into each shell. If desired, top with toasted slivered almonds. (See footnote on page 25 for toasting nuts.) Chill. Use leftover filling as spread for baking powder biscuits.

Pumpkin Filling: Bake tart shells at 400° for 10 to 12 minutes. Cool in pans. In saucepan combine ½ cup sugar, ¼ teaspoon *each* salt, ground cinnamon, ground ginger, and ground nutmeg; stir in 3 well-beaten eggs and 1 cup canned pumpkin. Cook and stir over low heat till thick, about 12 minutes. Remove from heat; chill. Fold in 1 cup frozen whipped dessert topping, thawed. Spoon about 2 teaspoons filling into each shell. Sprinkle with toasted chopped pecans. (See footnote on page 25 for toasting nuts.) Chill thoroughly. Serve leftover filling as pudding.

Pecan Filling: Beat together ¾ cup packed brown sugar, 1 egg, 1 tablespoon softened butter *or* margarine, 1 teaspoon vanilla, and dash salt *just till smooth*. Sprinkle ⅓ cup coarsely chopped pecans in *unbaked* tart shells. Divide filling among shells. Top with an additional ⅓ cup coarsely chopped pecans. Bake at 325° till set, about 25 minutes. Cool tarts in pans.

Almond Filling: Using ¼ cup raspberry preserves, spoon ½ teaspoon of the preserves into each *unbaked* tart shell. In mixing bowl combine ½ cup sugar and ¼ cup almond paste (2 ounces). Add 2 egg yolks, one at a time; beat well after each. Blend in 3 tablespoons all-purpose flour, 2 tablespoons light cream, and 1 tablespoon orange juice. Spoon a rounded teaspoonful of filling atop preserves in each tart shell. Bake at 400° for 15 minutes. Cool tarts in pans before removing.

Fruit Filling: In mixing bowl beat 1 egg; gradually beat in ¼ cup granulated sugar, ¼ cup packed brown sugar, and ⅛ teaspoon salt. Stir in ½ cup chopped walnuts; ½ cup chopped candied cherries; ½ cup raisins, chopped; 1 teaspoon shredded lemon peel; and 3 tablespoons lemon juice. Divide filling mixture among *unbaked* tart shells. Bake at 375° for 25 minutes. Cool tarts in pans.

Kringla

½ cup butter *or* margarine, softened
1¼ cups sugar
2 egg yolks
1 cup buttermilk
3 cups all-purpose flour
1 teaspoon baking powder
½ teaspoon baking soda
½ teaspoon salt
½ to 1 teaspoon ground cardamom

In mixing bowl cream butter and sugar till fluffy. Beat in egg yolks; blend in buttermilk. Stir flour with remaining ingredients. Add to creamed mixture; beat till well blended. Divide dough in half; wrap in waxed paper or clear plastic wrap. Chill thoroughly.

Divide one portion of the dough into 18 pieces. With hands, roll each piece of dough to a 9- or 10-inch rope on lightly floured surface. Shape each rope into a circle, crossing about 1½ inches from ends of rope. Twist rope at point where rope crosses. Seal ends of rope to center of opposite side of circle, forming a pretzel shape. Place on lightly greased cookie sheet. Repeat shaping with remaining dough. Bake at 375° till lightly browned on bottom, 12 to 14 minutes (tops will be pale). Makes 3 dozen cookies.

Capture the holiday spirit with a tempting refreshment of *Santa's Whiskers* and mugs of creamy eggnog. Flecked with candied cherries, the cookies are rolled in coconut to resemble the jolly old man's beard. Make them ahead, then slice and bake just before party time.

Krumkake

These crisp cookies are shown on pages 64 and 65 —

      3 eggs
    ½ cup sugar
    ½ cup butter, melted and cooled
    1 teaspoon vanilla
    ½ cup all-purpose flour

With rotary beater, beat eggs with sugar till thoroughly mixed. Blend in butter and vanilla. Beat in flour till smooth.

Heat krumkake iron on medium high heat. Make one cookie at a time. For 6-inch iron, drop *about ½ tablespoon* batter on hot, ungreased iron; close gently (do not squeeze). Bake over medium-high heat till light golden brown, 15 to 20 seconds. Turn iron over; bake 15 to 20 seconds. Loosen with knife and remove with spatula; immediately shape around wooden or metal roller. Reheat iron; repeat with remaining batter. Makes about 2 dozen.

Santa's Whiskers

      1 cup butter *or* margarine, softened
      1 cup sugar
      2 tablespoons milk
      1 teaspoon vanilla *or* rum flavoring
    2½ cups all-purpose flour
    ¾ cup finely chopped red *or* green
        candied cherries
    ½ cup finely chopped pecans
    ¾ cup flaked coconut

In mixing bowl cream together butter or margarine and sugar; blend in milk and vanilla or rum flavoring. Stir in flour, chopped candied cherries, and chopped pecans. Form dough into two 8-inch rolls. Roll in flaked coconut to coat outside. Wrap in waxed paper or clear plastic wrap; chill thoroughly.

Cut into ¼-inch slices. Place on ungreased cookie sheet. Bake at 375° till edges are golden, about 12 minutes. Makes about 60.

Christmas Card Cookies

Unusual gift cookies as shown on page 2—

> 1½ cups butter *or* margarine, softened
> 2 cups packed brown sugar
> 1 egg
> 4 cups all-purpose flour
> 2 teaspoons ground cinnamon
> 1 teaspoon ground nutmeg
> ½ teaspoon ground cloves
> ¼ teaspoon baking soda
>   Decorator icing

Cream butter and sugar; add egg. Beat till light and fluffy. Stir flour with spices and soda; add to creamed mixture. Mix well. Cover; chill till firm, about 2 hours.

For Giant Christmas Cards: For each cookie, roll ¾ *cup* of the dough to ¼-inch thickness directly on ungreased cookie sheet. Shape or cut into desired form: star, bell, circle, rectangle, or tree, keeping ¼ inch thick. Remove excess dough. Bake, one at a time, at 350° about 12 minutes. Cool 10 minutes; remove to rack to cool. Decorate as for Christmas cards, writing messages with decorator icing in desired colors. Let stand till icing is set before wrapping as gifts. Makes 6.

For Cookie Cutouts: On floured surface, roll dough to ⅛-inch thickness. Cut into desired shapes with cookie cutters. Place on ungreased cookie sheet. Bake at 350° till lightly browned, 8 to 10 minutes. Cool 1 to 2 minutes; remove to rack. If desired, decorate with decorator icing. Makes about 6 dozen.

TEST KITCHEN TIP

To shape *Stags' Antlers*, make two slits in each strip, cutting through a little more than half the width of the strip. Curve strip, opening slits to resemble antlers.

Candy Cane Cookies

Party-type cookies shown on pages 64 and 65—

> ¾ cup butter *or* margarine, softened
> ¾ cup sugar
> 1 egg
> ½ teaspoon vanilla
> ½ teaspoon peppermint extract
> 2 cups all-purpose flour
> ½ teaspoon salt
> ¼ teaspoon baking powder
> ⅓ cup flaked coconut
> 1 teaspoon red food coloring

Cream butter and sugar; beat in egg, vanilla, and extract. Stir flour with salt and baking powder; stir into creamed mixture. Divide dough in half. Stir coconut into one portion; blend food coloring into remaining dough. Cover; chill doughs for 30 minutes.

Divide *each* dough into 30 balls; keep half of each dough chilled till ready to use. With hands, roll each ball to a 5-inch rope. For each cane, pinch together one end of a red rope and one end of a white rope; twist ropes together. Pinch together remaining ends. Place on ungreased cookie sheet; curve to form cane. Repeat with remaining balls. Bake at 375° about 10 minutes. Makes 30.

Stags' Antlers

Lightly spiced with cardamom—

In mixing bowl cream together ½ cup softened butter *or* margarine and ¾ cup sugar. Beat in 2 egg yolks and 1 egg. Add ¼ cup milk and ½ teaspoon ground cardamom; mix thoroughly. Stir together 2¼ cups all-purpose flour, ½ cup cornstarch, 1 teaspoon baking soda, and ½ teaspoon salt. Add to creamed mixture; blend thoroughly. Cover dough and chill.

Divide dough in half. On lightly floured surface, roll *each* portion to a 12x6-inch rectangle. Cut into thirty-six 2x1-inch strips. Place on ungreased cookie sheets. In each strip, make 2 slits ¾ inch from each end, cutting slits a little more than half the width of the strip. Curve to open slits. Sprinkle with additional sugar. Bake at 350° till golden, 12 to 15 minutes. Cool on rack. Store in airtight container. Makes 6 dozen.

Snowmen Cookies

Cream 1 cup softened butter *or* margarine and ½ cup sifted powdered sugar; blend in 2 teaspoons vanilla. Stir 2 cups all-purpose flour with ½ teaspoon salt; add to creamed mixture. Blend well. Stir in 1 cup quick-cooking rolled oats. Divide dough in thirds.

Shape one part into twelve 1¼-inch balls (bases). Shape second part into twelve 1-inch balls (bodies). Shape third part into twelve ¾-inch balls (heads). Place on ungreased cookie sheets. Slightly flatten balls, *except* for smallest size. Bake at 325° till done, 15 to 20 minutes for small and medium balls, and 20 to 25 minutes for large balls. Cool. For icing, add enough light cream to 2 cups sifted powdered sugar for dipping consistency. Stir in dash salt and 1 teaspoon vanilla.

Dip each ball in icing, lifting out with fork to drain. Let dry. To make each snowman, fasten base, body, and head together with a little more icing. Decorate with red cinnamon candies, peppermint candies, gumdrops, small decorative candies, and licorice. Makes 12.

Fruit Nuggets

> 6 tablespoons butter *or* margarine, softened
> ¾ cup packed brown sugar
> 1 egg
> 2 tablespoons water
> 1½ cups all-purpose flour
> ½ teaspoon baking soda
> ¼ teaspoon salt
> ¼ teaspoon ground cinnamon
> ⅛ teaspoon ground cloves
> ½ cup raisins
> ½ cup chopped walnuts
> ½ cup chopped red and green candied cherries

Cream together butter or margarine and brown sugar. Add egg; beat well. Stir in water. Thoroughly stir together flour, baking soda, salt, cinnamon, and cloves; stir into creamed mixture. Mix in raisins, walnuts, and cherries. Spoon into individual tiny 1½-inch paper bake cups on cookie sheet. Bake at 375° for 9 to 10 minutes. Makes 6 dozen.

TEST KITCHEN TIP

For a uniform coating of icing on *Snowmen Cookies,* dip each ball into icing to completely cover. With fork, lift ball from icing, allowing excess to drip into bowl.

Black-Eyed Susans

Daisy-shaped cookies shown on pages 64 and 65—

> ¾ cup butter *or* margarine, softened
> 1¼ cups sugar
> 2 eggs
> 1 teaspoon orange extract
> 2½ cups all-purpose flour
> 1 teaspoon baking powder
> 1 teaspoon salt
> Orange Glaze
> Black gumdrops

Cream butter and sugar; beat in eggs and extract. Stir flour with baking powder and salt; stir into creamed mixture. Chill well.

Cut two daisy shapes from cardboard, one 3½ inches in diameter; one 2¼ inches in diameter. Or, use flower-shaped cookie cutters.

On lightly floured surface, roll *half* of the dough to ⅛-inch thickness; cut equal numbers of each flower size. Place on ungreased cookie sheets. Bake at 350° till done, 5 to 6 minutes for small flowers and 8 to 10 minutes for large flowers. Prepare Orange Glaze. Immediately brush over tops of baked cookies. Cool on rack. Repeat with remaining dough.

Add enough additional powdered sugar to remaining glaze to thicken; use to secure smaller flower to top of larger flower, staggering petal points. Center gumdrop atop each with a little glaze. Makes about 4 dozen.

Orange Glaze: Combine 2 cups sifted powdered sugar, ¼ cup milk, ½ teaspoon orange extract, and a few drops yellow food coloring.

Teatime Fancies

Brambles

¼ cup butter *or* margarine
1 slightly beaten egg
⅔ cup sugar
½ cup raisins
¼ cup finely crushed saltine
  crackers (about 7)
¼ cup lemon juice
  Pastry

Melt butter; cool. Mix with next 5 ingredients; set aside. Prepare Pastry; roll ⅛ inch thick. Cut into 3-inch rounds with floured biscuit cutter. Place in 1¾-inch muffin pans. Spoon about 1 tablespoon raisin filling in each. Bake at 400° for 15 to 18 minutes. Cool slightly; remove to rack. Makes 2 dozen.

Pastry: Stir 1½ cups all-purpose flour with ½ teaspoon salt. Cut in ½ cup shortening till size of small peas. Sprinkle 4 to 5 tablespoons cold water over all, one tablespoon at a time; toss after each addition. Form into a ball; flatten on lightly floured surface.

Chocolate Crinkles

1½ cups granulated sugar
½ cup cooking oil
3 1-ounce squares unsweetened
  chocolate, melted and cooled
2 teaspoons vanilla
3 eggs
¼ cup milk
2 cups all-purpose flour
2 teaspoons baking powder
  Sifted powdered sugar

Combine first 4 ingredients. Beat in eggs, one at a time; beat well after each. Stir in milk. Stir flour and baking powder together. Stir into egg mixture. Chill. Using 1 tablespoon dough for each, shape into balls; roll in powdered sugar. Place on greased cookie sheet. Bake at 375° for 10 to 12 minutes. While warm, roll again in powdered sugar. Makes 4 dozen.

Gumdrop Bars

Delicate orange icing caps these chewy bars flecked with gumdrops and pecans—

2 cups all-purpose flour
1 cup finely chopped gumdrops of
  assorted colors, *except* black
  (6 ounces)
½ cup chopped pecans
  • • •
4 eggs
1 tablespoon water
2 cups packed brown sugar
1 teaspoon ground cinnamon
¼ teaspoon salt
  • • •
3 tablespoons butter *or* margarine
1 teaspoon grated orange peel
2 tablespoons orange juice
  Sifted powdered sugar
  Sliced gumdrops

Thoroughly stir together flour, finely chopped gumdrops, and chopped pecans; set aside.

In medium bowl beat together eggs and water till foamy. Gradually add brown sugar, beating till mixture is light. Beat in cinnamon and salt. Stir gumdrop-flour mixture into brown sugar mixture. Spread in greased 15½x10½x 1-inch baking pan. Bake at 375° till cookies are done, 15 to 20 minutes.

Meanwhile, in saucepan melt butter or margarine over low heat. Remove from heat; stir in grated orange peel and orange juice. Stir in enough sifted powdered sugar to make a thin icing, blending till mixture is smooth. Spread icing over warm cookies. Cool; cut into bars. If desired, garnish each bar with a few sliced gumdrops. Makes 3 dozen.

Set the tea table with a variety of sweets for ▶ friends to enjoy as they sip and socialize. This setting offers a platter of raisin-rich *Brambles* and a tiered server stacked with divinity, *Gumdrop Bars*, and *Chocolate Crinkles*.

Brandy Snaps

Shaping requires practice, so use the first few cookies to develop your skill—

½ cup packed brown sugar
6 tablespoons butter *or* margarine, melted
¼ cup molasses
1 tablespoon brandy
¾ cup all-purpose flour
½ teaspoon ground ginger
½ teaspoon ground nutmeg
⅛ teaspoon salt
Dessert topping mix
Chopped candied ginger

In bowl combine brown sugar, melted butter or margarine, molasses, and brandy; mix well. Stir together flour, ground ginger, nutmeg, and salt. Stir into butter mixture.

Drop level teaspoonfuls of batter 4 inches apart on ungreased cookie sheet. Bake at 350° for 5 to 6 minutes. Cool 2 minutes on pan; remove with wide spatula. Immediately roll each cookie to form a cone, using metal cone for shaping. (If cookies harden before rolling, reheat in oven about 30 seconds.) Cool thoroughly; store in airtight container.

To serve, prepare dessert topping mix according to package directions. If desired, add a little additional brandy for flavor. Fold in chopped candied ginger. Spoon mixture into cones. (For softer cookies, fill with ginger-flavored dessert topping and refrigerate about an hour before serving.) Makes about 60.

TEST KITCHEN TIP

To shape *Brandy Snaps*, roll warm cookie around metal cone, then remove cone. Cookies will harden as they cool. If they cool before shaping, reheat in the oven.

Chocolate Waffle Drops

Waffle-shaped cookies shown on pages 64 and 65—

½ cup butter *or* margarine, softened
⅔ cup granulated sugar
2 eggs
1 teaspoon vanilla
1¼ cups all-purpose flour
¼ cup unsweetened cocoa powder
1 teaspoon baking powder
½ teaspoon salt
½ teaspoon ground cinnamon
½ cup chopped nuts
Powdered sugar

Cream butter and sugar till fluffy. Add eggs and vanilla; beat well. Stir together flour, cocoa, baking powder, salt, and cinnamon; stir into creamed mixture. Blend in nuts.

Drop by teaspoon 2 inches apart on preheated waffle baker; bake till done, about 1 minute.* Remove to rack to cool. Sift powdered sugar over cookies. Makes about 48.

*Or, drop dough by teaspoon 2 inches apart on lightly greased cookie sheet. Bake at 350° till cookies are done, 10 to 12 minutes.

Vanilla Waffle Drops: Prepare Chocolate Waffle Drops *except* omit cocoa and cinnamon. Bake for 1½ to 2 minutes.

Cream Cheese Dainties

½ cup butter *or* margarine, softened
1 3-ounce package cream cheese, softened
½ cup sugar
¼ teaspoon almond extract
1 cup all-purpose flour
2 teaspoons baking powder
¼ teaspoon salt
1½ cups crisp rice cereal, coarsely crushed
Red and green candied cherries

Cream together first 4 ingredients. Stir flour with baking powder and ¼ teaspoon salt; stir into creamed mixture just till combined. Chill 1 to 2 hours. Form into balls; roll in cereal. Place on ungreased cookie sheet. Top each with a cherry, pressing in lightly. Bake at 350° for 12 to 15 minutes. Cool. Makes 48.

Mint Meltaways

1 cup butter *or* margarine, softened
1 cup crushed butter mints
    (about 5 ounces)
2 cups all-purpose flour
1 tablespoon sugar

In small mixer bowl cream butter at medium speed of electric mixer till light and fluffy. Add mints; mix well. Add flour; blend well at low speed. Cover; chill for 1 hour.

On waxed paper, roll or pat chilled dough to a 9-inch square. Sprinkle dough with sugar. Cut into 1½-inch squares. Place on ungreased cookie sheet. Using a small cookie cutter or floured thimble, lightly press a design on the surface of each square of dough. Bake at 325° till pale golden brown, 15 to 18 minutes. Do not overbake. Makes 3 dozen.

Ginger Strips

Use any fruit preserves you have on hand—

1 cup shortening
1 cup sugar
2 eggs
½ cup light molasses
1 teaspoon grated orange peel
3 cups all-purpose flour
1 teaspoon ground cinnamon
1 teaspoon ground ginger
1 teaspoon salt
½ teaspoon ground cloves
    Preserves *or* sugar

Cream shortening and 1 cup sugar till fluffy. Add eggs, one at a time; beat well after each. Blend in molasses and peel. Stir flour with cinnamon, ginger, salt, and cloves. Stir into creamed mixture, mixing well.

Spread dough in ten 14x1½-inch strips on greased cookie sheets.* Using back of spoon, make indentation the length of each strip. Fill with preserves or sprinkle with a little sugar. Bake at 375° till done, 10 to 12 minutes for soft cookies and 15 to 17 minutes for crisp cookies. While warm, cut each strip diagonally into 12 cookies. Makes 10 dozen.

*Or, drop from teaspoon on greased cookie sheet. Sprinkle with sugar; bake as above.

TEST KITCHEN TIP

Use a small cookie cutter to imprint decorative designs in *Mint Meltaways*. Make a shallow cut in top of each cookie with cutter, being careful not to cut too deep.

Cameo Cookies

½ cup butter *or* margarine, softened
1 cup sugar
1 egg
¼ cup milk
½ teaspoon vanilla
¼ teaspoon lemon extract
• • •
2¼ cups all-purpose flour
2 teaspoons baking powder
½ teaspoon salt
    Chocolate Spritz

Cream butter and sugar; blend in egg, milk, and flavorings. Stir flour with baking powder and salt; stir into batter. Chill 1 hour.

Prepare, but do *not* bake, Chocolate Spritz. On lightly floured surface, roll chilled sugar cookie dough to ¼-inch thickness; cut into rounds with 2-inch cookie cutter. Place rounds on ungreased cookie sheet. With spatula, carefully place a chilled spritz atop each sugar cookie round. Bake at 400° for 10 to 12 minutes. Makes about 6½ dozen.

Chocolate Spritz: Cream 1 cup softened butter *or* margarine and 1 cup sugar till fluffy; beat in 1 egg. Blend in two 1-ounce squares unsweetened chocolate, melted and cooled, and 1 teaspoon vanilla. Stir together 2 cups all-purpose flour and ½ teaspoon salt; add to creamed mixture, mixing thoroughly. Pack dough, *half* at a time, in cookie press. Press into desired shapes on ungreased cookie sheet; chill unbaked cookies till firm, 10 to 15 minutes.

Prune Bars

    Prune Filling
  1 **cup all-purpose flour**
  1 **cup quick-cooking rolled oats**
  ½ **cup packed brown sugar**
  ½ **teaspoon ground cinnamon**
  ½ **cup butter** *or* **margarine**

Prepare Prune Filling; cool. Mix flour, oats, sugar, and cinnamon. Cut in butter till crumbly; mix well. Pat *half* of the oat mixture in greased 9x9x2-inch baking pan. Spread with filling. Crumble remaining oat mixture over top; press lightly into filling. Bake at 350° for 30 to 35 minutes. Cool; cut into bars. Makes 24.

  Prune Filling: Add enough water to ½ of a 6-ounce can frozen lemonade concentrate, thawed (6 tablespoons) to make 1 cup liquid. In saucepan simmer 1 cup snipped, pitted prunes (6 ounces), covered, in lemonade mixture till tender, 4 to 5 minutes. Mix ½ cup packed brown sugar, ⅓ cup chopped walnuts, 2 tablespoons all-purpose flour, and ⅛ teaspoon salt; add to prune mixture. Cook and stir till very thick, about 5 minutes.

Cheery Cherry Cookies

In mixing bowl cream together ¾ cup softened butter *or* margarine and ¾ cup sugar till light and fluffy. Beat in 1 egg and ¼ cup cherry preserves. Thoroughly stir together 2¼ cups all-purpose flour, 1 teaspoon baking soda, and ½ teaspoon salt. Blend dry ingredients into creamed mixture, mixing thoroughly.

  Drop dough from teaspoon 2 inches apart on ungreased cookie sheet. Bake at 375° till lightly browned, 8 to 10 minutes. Let cool on cookie sheet 1 to 2 minutes before removing to rack. Spoon a little additional cherry preserves atop each cookie; top with a blanched almond half. Makes 4 dozen.

◄ **Decorative and dainty,** these tea morsels include *Prune Bars* topped with crumbs, *Cheery Cherry Cookies* dotted with preserves and nuts, *Mexican Mocha Balls* rolled in extra-fine sugar, and *Jam Thumbprints* wreathed with meringue.

Jam Thumbprints

  ¾ **cup butter** *or* **margarine, softened**
  ½ **cup sugar**
  2 **eggs**
  1½ **teaspoons vanilla**
  2 **cups all-purpose flour**
  1½ **teaspoons baking powder**
  ¼ **teaspoon salt**
  ½ **cup red raspberry, boysenberry,** *or* **currant jam**
  ⅓ **cup chopped filberts**
  1 **teaspoon grated orange** *or* **lemon peel**
  2 **egg whites**
  ¼ **teaspoon cream of tartar**
  ½ **cup sugar**

Cream first 2 ingredients. Add eggs and vanilla; beat well. Stir flour with baking powder and salt; stir into creamed mixture. Chill at least 1 hour. Shape into 48 balls. Place 2 inches apart on greased cookie sheet. With moistened finger, make indentation atop each ball. Mix jam, nuts, and peel. Fill indentations with ½ *teaspoon* of the jam filling.

  Beat egg whites with cream of tartar till soft peaks form. Gradually add ½ cup sugar; beat to stiff peaks. Pipe a wreath of meringue around jam atop each ball. Bake at 350° for 10 to 13 minutes. Makes 4 dozen.

Mexican Mocha Balls

  1 **cup butter** *or* **margarine, softened**
  ½ **cup granulated sugar**
  1 **teaspoon vanilla**
  2 **cups all-purpose flour**
  ¼ **cup unsweetened cocoa powder**
  1 **teaspoon instant coffee crystals**
  ¼ **teaspoon salt**
  1 **cup finely chopped walnuts**
  ½ **cup chopped maraschino cherries**
  Extra-fine granulated sugar

Cream first 3 ingredients. Stir flour with cocoa, coffee, and salt. Gradually beat into creamed mixture. Stir in nuts and cherries. Chill 1 hour. Form into 1-inch balls. Place on ungreased baking sheet. Bake at 325° for 20 minutes. Cool on rack. While warm but not hot, dust with extra-fine sugar. Makes 84.

Making and Giving Cookies

Following a recipe isn't the only secret to cookie-making success. Being familiar with cookie types, decorating with flair, and storing properly are all important in a winning cookie game.

To select the cookie you want to make, it helps to know what basic preparation is involved. The do's and don'ts of each cookie type serve as guidelines for tasty cookies every time. After the cookies are baked, you can brighten many of them with color by adding simple decorative touches such as sugar and frostings. Once decorated, make sure to store your homemade specialties correctly to ensure freshness.

Your family loves a batch of fresh cookies, and so do others. So, why not give those delectable morsels as gifts to the special people in your life? Even friends who live far away can enjoy cookie gifts sent by mail. It's a simple way to show you care.

Surprise a friend with one of these cookies (clockwise, starting at top left): *Butter Pecan Cookies, Nut Crescents, Chocolate-Oatmeal Cookies, Almond-Coconut Bars, Frosted Pecan Bars,* and *German Chocolate Brownies.* (See Index for page numbers.)

Selecting, Decorating, and Storing Cookies

Cookies come in an endless choice of types and shapes. To categorize the wide array, they have been divided by the stiffness of dough and the way in which they are handled. Regardless of the category, most cookies may be baked ahead if properly stored to keep their fresh-from-the-oven flavor.

Types of Cookies

Bar Cookies: A cross between a cake and a cookie, bar cookies are baked in a pan. As a rule, they are then cooled and cut into bars, squares, or diamonds. The unbaked dough is usually stiff and must be spread or patted into the pan. After baking, the bars should have a thin, delicate crust and a moist crumb. Over-mixing produces a hard and crusty top; over-baking results in a dry and crumbly cookie.

Bake fudge-like bars till the cookies appear dull and a slight imprint remains after touching the surface with a fingertip. Test cake-like bars for doneness with a wooden pick.

Drop Cookies: Named after the way they're formed on the cookie sheet, the dough for drop cookies is soft, usually mounds when dropped, then flattens slightly during baking. Be sure to allow for some spreading of the dough. To prevent cookies from spreading too much during baking, drop dough onto a cooled cookie sheet, mounding dough slightly.

Drop cookies are properly baked when lightly browned and a soft imprint remains after touching with a fingertip. Overbaked drop cookies will be dark and crisp; under-baked cookies will be doughy.

Refrigerator Cookies: Have freshly baked cookies at a moment's notice when you keep tightly wrapped rolls of refrigerator cookie dough on hand in your refrigerator or freezer. Store unbaked dough in the refrigerator for up to one week or in the freezer for up to six months.

Be sure the dough is thoroughly chilled before slicing and baking. Use a back-and-forth sawing motion when slicing cookies to retain the shape. For extra-crisp cookies, slice thin; bake till lightly browned.

Rolled Cookies: Cutout cookie dough is stiff enough to be rolled out, then cut into assorted shapes. For easier handling, chill the dough before rolling and work with small amounts at a time, keeping remaining chilled till needed. Unchilled dough takes up too much flour, resulting in tough, dry cookies. Excessive rerolling also causes tough cookies.

Use a knife, cookie cutters, or traceable cardboard patterns to produce unusual cookie designs. Bake till lightly browned.

Shaped Cookies: Included are cookies formed by hand into assorted shapes and those forced through a cookie press. Cookies shaped by hand usually are molded into small balls or rolled into pencil-shaped ropes and then formed into various designs, such as wreaths or pretzels. Some cookies retain their shape during baking, while others flatten slightly and become crinkly on top.

To use a press for shaping cookies, follow the manufacturer's directions.

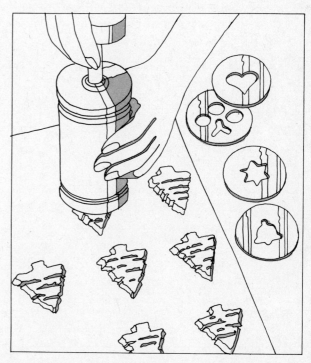

Adding a Decorative Note

Frostings: Consider the flavor and type of cookie when adding a frosting trim. Since frostings add sweetness and richness, remember to choose one that is compatible with the cookie flavor, then frost sparingly.

To dress up bar cookies, spread with frosting or drizzle with confectioner's icing or a thin chocolate glaze. For drop cookies, spoon a dollop of frosting atop each. Use frosting as a filling to hold refrigerator cookies together sandwich-style. For children's parties, pipe decorator's icing on cutout cookies.

Sugars: One of the simplest cookie trims is a sprinkling or coating of sugar. Use powdered sugar, granulated sugar, or colored sugar crystals on various cookie types. Sliced, dropped, or rolled cookies can be sprinkled with granulated or colored sugar before baking. For molded cookies, roll unbaked balls in granulated sugar or flatten them with the bottom of a glass dipped in sugar. To decorate baked cookies, sift powdered sugar over cookies or shake in sifted powdered sugar. Repeat shaking for heavier coating.

Jams and jellies: Provide a colorful topping or an instant filling for cookies with jams and jellies. Fill cookies just before serving, since jams become tacky on standing and may soften a crisp cookie.

Use jams and jellies as a filling for cutout cookies or to assemble plain cookies sandwich-style. Frost drop cookies with a dollop of preserves or spread rolled cookies with a thin layer of jelly. Make a thumbprint in shaped cookie balls before baking, then fill the indentation with jam or jelly after baking.

Nuts, fruits, and candies: Some of the cookie-making ingredients also are versatile toppings. They are suitable for decorating almost all types of cookies and may be used to add crunch, flavor, or color.

Roll cookies in finely chopped nuts or top with nut halves before baking; when cookies are done, the nuts will have a toasted flavor and will stick to the cookies. Another time, decorate cookies with maraschino cherries, raisins, coconut, dates, candied fruits or peels, sliced gumdrops, or decorative candies.

Storing for Freshness

For short-time storage: Remember when storing cookies not to mix soft and crisp varieties in the same container, or the crisp types will soon become soft. Store most cookies in tightly covered containers, such as a plastic or metal container with a sealable cover or a canister with a snug lid. Soft cookies can be stored in loosely covered containers.

To add moisture to soft cookies that have begun to dry out, place an apple half, skin side down, atop cookies in storage container. Remove and discard fruit after a day or two. Store cookies with very moist fillings in a loosely covered container. Refrigerate if desired. For ease, store bar cookies in the pan in which they were baked; cover pan tightly.

For longer storage: Freeze *baked* cookies in freezer containers, freezer bags, or foil for up to 12 months. (Always pack fragile cookies in freezer containers.) Before serving, thaw in freezer wrappings. To freeze *unbaked* cookies, pack dough into freezer containers or shape stiff dough into rolls and wrap securely in foil. Freeze up to 6 months.

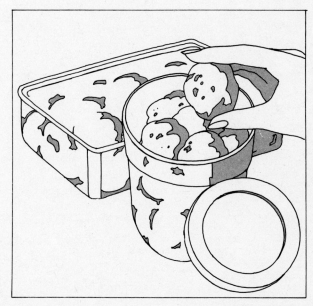

Giving Cookies as Gifts

Baking cookies is twice the fun when you share them with someone else. Whether it's a special occasion such as Christmas or a birthday, or just an ordinary weekday, presenting an assortment of home-baked cookies to a friend or relative brightens the day for both of you. A wide variety of cookies especially good for giving are listed on page 90.

Once the cookies are baked, don't stop there. Make your gift even more impressive by delivering it in an inventive carryall that shows some extra thought. Try constructing decorative boxes such as those shown on the opposite page. By following the directions you can create boxes to fit any occasion.

If time doesn't allow for handcrafted boxes, take a look around the house for container ideas. Your kitchen holds a variety of suitable cookie carriers that are useful long after the last crumbs are eaten. Conventional pans, jars, and bowls make unusual and inexpensive gifts when filled with confections. Keep this in mind on the next trip to the store. A new neighbor will appreciate a baking pan or a colorful glass pitcher, especially if cookies go along with the house-warming gift. At a wedding shower, bestow a future homemaker with a bread board stacked with bar cookies. Don't forget to include the recipe. Choosing containers such as decorated coffee cans, bright paper plates, and colorful baskets completes your cookie gift in a practical way, too.

Holiday Gifts

Let the calendar serve as a reminder for baking and giving cookie gifts. From January to December, a host of holidays offer the perfect opportunity to give timely kitchen treats to special people.

Start the celebrating of any holiday of the year by giving cookies that are sure to please all ages. An adult will enjoy Cherry-Almond Bars (see recipe, page 16) on George Washington's birthday just as much as small trick-or-treaters love cookie treats at Halloween. Add a few drops of green food coloring to plain cookie dough for a St. Patrick's Day gift. For a different approach to Easter tradition, try filling egg baskets with cookies. Baskets of cookies on May Day are also a thoughtful gesture. Don't overlook cookies as a bang-up gift on the 4th of July. If you're celebrating away from home, simply tote the cookies along. They are a universal holiday food.

The Christmas season is a natural for gift giving, so include cookies on your holiday gift list. Wrap them as you would any present and set them under the tree or hand deliver to friends with best wishes. Cookies will be an even more welcome delight when transported in festive handmade gift boxes. With a little imagination, you can design containers in any shape or size. To spark the Christmas spirit, a cookie gift exchange is a great way to herald the holiday season. Each person brings a favorite type of cookie to share and then takes home an assortment to enjoy. Some of the cookies can even be used to decorate the Christmas tree.

Birthday Gifts

When giving the best is important, make it cookies for a birthday wish that tastes great. Surprise a special friend or relative with something from the oven the next time you're baffled for a gift idea. It's a simple, friendly way to show you care. If the birthday person lives far away, don't let the distance discourage good intentions. Send the cookies via mail. They'll arrive looking homemade fresh if you follow the suggestions under Packing for Faraway Places on page 91.

Although birthdays are traditionally celebrated with cake, cookies are also worthy of a party. For example, plan an afternoon coffee for a neighbor's birthday, and have each invited guest bring a plate of her favorite cookies. Add a pot of coffee for an instant party that makes the day. Cookies also can be a big hit at children's parties when packed in miniature boxes for each little guest to take home. You might try cookies for game prizes, too.

Delightful to give as well as to receive, *Sweet Chocolate Cookies,* pecan-topped *Orange Drop Cookies,* and *Saucepan Taffy Bars* are dressed up in easy-to-make gift boxes. (See below for directions on making the gift boxes, see Index for recipe page numbers.)

Directions for Making Gift Boxes

Cardboard Boxes: To make cardboard boxes shown above, assemble the following supplies: sharp knife or single-edged razor blade, lightweight cardboard, spray paints, model cement, shoestrings, leather, wooden beads, felt or cotton braid, large needle, heavy-duty thread, and self-adhesive decals.

Using the knife or razor blade, cut box pieces from cardboard in desired shapes and sizes. (To prevent accidents, wrap the short horizontal edge of the blade with adhesive tape.) Color cardboard pieces with bright spray paint, using a contrasting color for the inside of boxes. Let dry.

Assemble box pieces, using modeling cement to hold seams. Shoestrings or leather loops hook around wooden beads to serve as fasteners. Make handles from felt, shoestring, or cotton braid attached with glue or sewn in place. Trim boxes with self-adhesive decals and other materials.

Clay Boxes: To make the tower-style boxes shown on page 70, assemble the following supplies: rolling pin, ready-to-bake modeling compound, cookie sheets, sharp knife or cookie cutters, orange stick, white glue, water-base paint, and clear lacquer.

Using rolling pin, roll modeling "clay" into four 8x4-inch rectangles (sides of box) and one 4-inch square (bottom of box). Place rectangles and square on cookie sheets. Use sharp knife or cookie cutters to make assorted small cutout designs in rectangles. Use orange stick to mark decorative indentations on rectangles (do not cut through). Bake all pieces at 350° for 15 minutes. Cool.

To assemble box, glue the baked and cooled rectangles together lengthwise along the edges. At one end glue square along edges of rectangles, forming bottom of box. Spray box with paint. Dry thoroughly, then seal with lacquer.

Gift Cookies

Anyday Gifts

Although gifts are mainly associated with holidays and birthdays, there's no reason why you can't make an ordinary day more memorable by giving a gift of cookies. Your gifts are often more meaningful when delivered on an impromptu basis anyway. Welcome a neighbor home from vacation or honor a tennis champ.

Hobbies provide clues for personalized cookies, which are guaranteed smile-makers. Flower-shaped cookies are an excellent selection for an avid gardener. Cookies cut in the shape of a football make a novel gift for a high school athlete who scored a winning touchdown. To make a particular shape, prepare rolled cookie dough and cut with cookie cutters or cardboard patterns. Add a bit of frosting to create the original gift.

Try writing messages on Christmas Card Cookies (see recipe, page 74) for a clever gift, rather than sending a card. Or vary the shape and the greeting for get-well wishes for a shut-in friend or congratulations to a graduate. Inscribe greetings with colored frostings. Your kindhearted words are twice as sweet when written on cookies.

Cookie gifts, however, need not always be fancy or clever. In Grandmother's day, a borrowed pan or dish was never returned empty but was delivered with cookies inside as a thank-you. Cookie gifts such as these carry feelings of goodwill without making the recipient feel indebted.

Kids and cookies go together like peanut butter and jelly. Children love such all-time favorites as chocolate chip cookies. Homemade cookies are a comforting sign from home when sent to a child away at camp or tucked in a suitcase before going on a trip. Whatever the reason for your cookie gift to a child, he'll feel the warmth of friendship in every chewy bite. If possible, deliver the cookies in a container the child can use later on, such as a toy dump truck.

Children also love to make cookie gifts themselves. They'll learn to measure and bake as they have fun creating gifts for grandparents, teachers, and classmates. Have them start with some of the easier cereal cookies and before you know it, they'll be rolling, cutting, and decorating cookies like pros.

Packing for Faraway Places

Receiving cookies in the mail is one of the little joys of life. However, the thrill is quickly crushed if, upon opening the box, only crumbs remain. Prevent this disaster from happening to your gift of cookies by following these suggestions for careful mailing:

First, select cookies that are mailable. Soft, moist cookies generally travel best. Avoid sending fragile or brittle cookies, such as sugar cookies. Bar cookies, brownies, and drop cookies are least likely to be damaged because they are more sturdy. Also, eliminate those with moist fillings or frostings, as they may become sticky at room temperature. For some suggestions of cookies that travel well, see the list of favorites in the next column.

Second, choose a durable cardboard box or metal container for packing. Line the container with waxed paper, foil, or plastic wrap. Then, place a layer of the same material or crumpled newspaper on the bottom. Do not use popped popcorn or puffed cereal for packing material, as it may attract insects.

Third, pack cookies properly inside the box for extra protection. Wrap them individually or back-to-back in pairs, using plastic wrap or foil. Place the wrapped cookies in snug rows inside the packing box or container. Between each layer of cookies, place a cushion of crumpled waxed paper, newspaper, or paper toweling. Remember that cookies can be crushed when they have room to move inside the box. Don't forget a final layer of cushioning material at the top of the box.

If desired, you can leave bar cookies in a foil pan for mailing as long as the pan is cushioned inside the box with newspaper or paper toweling. Make sure the cookies are tightly covered with a lid or with foil taped to the pan. Metal containers also should be well packed and cushioned in a box.

Finally, tape the outer box shut securely. Wrap in mailing paper and tie with string. Clearly label with addresses of both the receiver and sender. Write "Fragile, Handle with Care" on both sides of the box. You may also request special handling by the postal service.

Good Travelers

BAR COOKIE ARITHMETIC

Bar cookies may be cut into a variety of shapes and sizes. The number of bars a recipe yields depends on the size of the pan as well as the size of the portion. As a general rule, the thicker the bar, the smaller it should be cut. Likewise, the richer the bar, the smaller the serving. Use the table below as a guide for cutting bar cookies. Although only one yield is given in each recipe, you can vary the number of bars by looking at the pan size and cutting as desired.

Note: For special occasions, bar cookies can be cut into diamond shapes by making diagonal cuts in one direction and cuts straight across in the other direction. The yield will be slightly less.

Baking Pan Size	Number of Cuts Lengthwise	Crosswise	Approximate Size of Bar	Number of Bars
8x8x2-inch	3	3	2x2-inch	16
	3	4	2x1⅝-inch	20
	3	5	2x1⅜-inch	24
	3	6	2x1⅛-inch	28
	3	7	2x1-inch	32
11x7½x1½-inch	3	3	1⅞x2¾-inch	16
	4	3	1½x2¾-inch	20
	5	3	1¼x2¾-inch	24
	6	3	1x2¾-inch	28
	3	7	1⅞x1⅜-inch	32
9x9x2-inch	2	5	3x1½-inch	18
	3	4	2¼x1¾-inch	20
	3	5	2¼x1½-inch	24
	3	7	2¼x1⅛-inch	32
	5	5	1½x1½-inch	36
13x9x2-inch	2	7	3x1⅝-inch	24
	3	7	2¼x1⅝-inch	32
	5	5	1½x2⅛-inch	36
	7	4	1⅛x2⅝-inch	40
	7	5	1⅛x2⅛-inch	48
15½x10½x1-inch	3	8	2⅝x1¾-inch	36
	3	11	2⅝x1¼-inch	48
	3	14	2⅝x1-inch	60
	7	7	1¼x2-inch	64
	7	8	1¼x1¾-inch	72

INDEX

D-F

Have BETTER HOMES AND GAR-DENS® magazine delivered to your door. For information, write to: MR. ROBERT AUSTIN, P.O. BOX 4536, DES MOINES, IA 50336.